WIRED

Connect
with what
makes you
come alive

Jill Chambers

Wired
© 2021 by Jill Chambers

Published by Insight International, Inc.
contact@freshword.com
www.freshword.com
918-493-1718

ISBN: 978-1-943361-80-9
E-Book ISBN: 978-1-943361-81-6

Library of Congress Control Number: 2020924513

Printed in the United States of America.

ENDORSEMENTS

"Jill Chambers has written a vividly clear blueprint to understanding personal behavior and unveiled a great strategy to strengthen connections with others. Through her brilliant mix of personal experiences and behavioral science, *Wired* will undoubtedly change the lens in which life is seen and empower you to take back control of your behavior, making a positive impact on your life."

> —Nathan Gooden
> CFO, Amazon Echo Alexa

"Jill Chambers understands that discovering our purpose is vital to our daily lives, healthy relationships, and faith in God. Drawing on the DISC system, her own experience, and proven biblical wisdom, *Wired* reveals the connections between the way God made us and His purpose for our lives. Highly recommended!"

> —Chris Hodges
> Senior Pastor, Church of the Highlands
> Author of *The Daniel Dilemma* and
> *Out of the Cave*

"This book is a one-stop shop for improving yourself and all your relationships with humans. It's like having X-ray vision into the internal wiring of yourself and others. Suddenly you understand why they act the way they do, which helps you respond differently to them while still being true to yourself. I have personally seen relationships of all kinds (marriages, business partners, coworkers, etc.,) restored and renewed because of what Jill teaches here. Read it, live it, and you'll love it!"

> —Kerry Morris, CFP®, CFEd®
> Cofounder, Assurance Financial
> Partners, LLC

"This book is loaded with wisdom that will help you enhance your ability to see others and, in turn, help inspire them and move them into alignment with their utmost potential. Jill presents a practical approach to help individuals at all levels of any organization to get the most out of the people supporting them and help the entire team reach their God-given potential."

—Dr. Jason Kestner, DC
CEO of Kestner Health + Wellness

"As a transition specialist and coach, it is my job to engage professionally and personally with administrators and teachers in our three hundred child-development schools in eleven states. Diving into *Wired* has challenged and changed the way I connect. *Wired* proves the way we relate to an individual is unique to them; how we converse and body language is specific to them. Reading *Wired* has caused me to create stronger bonds between administrators, their teachers, and the children they care for."

—Paula Lugrand Martin
Childcare Network, Inc.
Transition Specialist and Coach

"In my fourth year of pastoring, I was challenged with getting the right people in the right seats on the bus, and with having congregants actually living out their personal mission statements. Meeting Jill Chambers changed everything! Our ministry teams are stronger, and our work now extends into seven nations."

—Bishop Tony Dunn
New Day Global Network
Tonydunn.org

"As a health-care academic and professional of thirty-five years, I have had numerous opportunities to participate and learn from 360° leadership and personality-type experiences and training. So with that background, I find *Wired* by Jill Chambers to be refreshing in her approach to frame DISC personality types from the individual's many life personas we all navigate each day, such as "at work" or "at home." For me, it was revealing to learn that my "at work" DISC personality type is D-47 C-29 I-26 S-18, while my "at home" DISC personality type is C-41 D-35 S-24 I-20, which clarifies some of the conflicts I experience when transitioning from one situation to the other. Thank you, Jill, for bringing this omitted fact to my attention in *Wired*."

—Dr. Chester Lynn Hurst
DDS, MS, FACD
Cofounder and Chief Dental Officer
of Candid™
Founder and CEO of SmileRx

DEDICATION

In loving memory of my Happily Ever After, Danny. Thank you for filling my heart and my coffee and for making sure I came up for air. Your belief in me and my passion for people was the fuel that helped me cross the finish line.

CONTENTS

FOREWORD

From the moment I met Jill Chambers in 1999, I knew she was special. Her passion for people captured my heart. Her intrigue of behavioral science made it very clear that she would be one for me to mentor in this field. Completing the DISC certification in 2000 through the Institute for Motivational Living, which I founded, she began immediately to utilize the resources and tools now in her tool belt. Deepening self-awareness and strengthening relationships in all circles from marriage, family, church, education, and business has been both her passion and gift, producing incredible results.

I have experienced her teaching in workshops, and have witnessed her utilizing the principles in this book to navigate uncomfortable tension in business and board meetings. She has a unique gift to direct a symphony of personalities and behavioral styles. Now to witness her become an author brings my heart great joy, as she has much wisdom and life experiences to share.

Wired will not only enlighten you to better understand yourself, but it will also inspire you to crave the understanding of others as never before. When we understand one another, we can find agreement. Where there's agreement, there's power.

This book is timely as we continue to navigate a world under stress. You are certain to laugh as you dive into the many adventures of this charming behavioral consultant. Get ready for your mind to be stretched and your heart to be awakened. You, my friend, have chosen wisely. *Wired* will change your life for the better and empower you to live your best life.

—Dr. Sandy Kulkin, PhD
Founder, Institute for
Motivational Living

ACKNOWLEDGMENTS

Special thanks to . . .

Mom and Dad, for your unconditional love and powerful words of wisdom throughout my life.

My Tribe of Five: Melody, Christopher, Sydni, Isaac, and Destiny. I am certainly the most blessed among mothers to have such amazing children. Not only are you brave and strong, but you are also kind, loving, and generous. I couldn't be more proud of the stunning humans you continue to become. Your willingness and patience during my experimental assessments allowed me to grow and gave me the best examples for this book. Thank you for believing in me and for cheering me all the way to the finish line. I love each of you and your families ferociously.

Melissa, for always inspiring me to be the best big sister I can be.

Mom-Darlene, for your love and support.

Paula, for laughing with me, crying with me, and just being there.

Sandy and Patty, for teaching me your Jedi behavioral science ways and treating me like your own.

Craig, for a lifetime of encouragement, support, and prayers.

Cyndi, for helping me dot my i's and cross my t's.

My Oasis family, for twenty-two years of life-giving community that I will forever cherish.

CHAPTER ONE

Your Wonderful Wiring

Life, if you will, is like a puzzle—and each of us are pieces of that puzzle. Much of our lives are spent looking for our place in the puzzle—our purpose. And yet for many, much time is wasted trying to fit where we don't belong. We try to be like other pieces rather than being the piece of the puzzle only we can be. The only way the puzzle can be completed is for each piece—each person—to be who we were designed to be.

Many spend their entire lives admiring the shapes of other pieces and comparing themselves, only to be constantly disappointed. When you get caught up in the trap of comparison, you'll only find yourself in one of two places: Comparison will leave you feeling devalued as you compare yourself to others and their strengths. Or it will keep you full of pride as you see your own strengths and elevate yourself above others and their limitations. The truth is that you are always less than some and better than others. You have less education, less money, and fewer friends. Or you have more. To end this vicious cycle, you need to recognize that the one person you need to compare yourself with is the person in the mirror. Each day, look deep into your reflection and ask yourself, *Am I the best version of me? Am I better today than I was yesterday?*

Are you becoming better each day?

Identifying your own piece to this puzzle of life is essential to feeling like you are where you belong. It gives you a sense of knowing that this is exactly who you are and where you need to be. So, the question is this: *How can we really know who we were made to be?* We are all wired differently. We all think differently. Remember the one person in your class in school who always had their hand up, ready to answer the question or give their opinion and input? And the class clown who never seemed to receive affirmation for the creative way they kept the morale of the class high through their humorous interruptions? They were usually late to class or barely sliding in at the ring of the bell. And thank God for those who always had extra pens and paper and were willing to share without expecting anything in return. They were the ones ready to help when you couldn't seem to find the proper answer to that mathematical problem.

Then there were those who arrived early to class because they determinedly kept their head down as they passed through the halls so they wouldn't feel obligated to stop and talk to anyone. After all, who has time to socialize in between classes? They had to arrive early and maintain their perfect record.

Even at an early age, our behavior can be identified. In fact, if misunderstood, our behavior will constantly be corrected and devalued, leaving us void and feeling like we need to be something we were never wired to be. When you identify that your behavior is a result of your thinking and your thinking is the result of the way you were wired, you will feel empowered to take control of your life rather than feel controlled by your thinking and behavior.

While there are many tools and resources that assist in self-discovery, I'm a strong advocate for a personality identifier called DISC—built around four primary emotions and the forms of behavior that flow from them. We are going to look at the basics of the DISC personality identifier and each of the four types. I'll explain how each of the emotions and behaviors in these four types function in our actions—usually through unconscious and long-ingrained responses. Most of us are a combination of these four types, which can often bring a sense of confusion when identifying our behavioral style. Don't worry, help is on the way. You are embarking on a great adventure, the discovery of you and how you are wired.

Although I had known about and studied DISC and had consequently put an understanding of human emotional responses into practice, the *ah ha!* experience that showed me how practical my actions were in light of my understanding of DISC came in the time of a great disaster in my city. Then I saw clearly the great value of each person functioning the way they were made and the positive results in the lives of many people that came about from this.

It all started with two days of rain.

In May 2010, Nashville was hit with one of the most severe floods in Tennessee history. Nashville shattered nearly every rainfall record; according to the National Weather Service, 13.57 inches of rain fell in two days. Approximately 11,000 properties were damaged or destroyed in the flood, more than 10,000 people were displaced from their homes, and a number of people died. One TV channel referred to it as the 1,000-year flood. Most homeowners in our town did not have flood insurance. It was not something that was on our radar in the areas of the city that were affected. Many found themselves overwhelmed by the damage, confusion, and chaos.

At that time my husband, Danny, and I were leading a very large church just outside Nashville. In efforts to help serve our city, we called for volunteers to step out of their comfort zones and go into the communities that had experienced severe damage to see how we could help. My heart is so passionate about helping others that I went into a community just a few miles from my home and began to canvass the neighborhood, assessing damages and seeking wisdom on how we could help these families. I learned that without flood insurance, residents themselves had to remove all the water-damaged flooring and walls before mold set in and made things even worse.

The first day our volunteers went in, I noticed that the homeowners were overwhelmed. As we offered assistance in cleaning up from the flood damage, several did not even know how to direct us. They were in shock. A few homeowners knew precisely what to do and led us with great clarity. The very first home I went into with a team was one of these. I learned from those homeowners how to remove the flooring, bleach the walls, and set dryers around to kill any mold that was attempting to develop from the moisture. They were so organized and thorough. We had the home to a place of drying out by the end of the day.

It was after this experience that I realized I needed to develop a strategy to best serve this community based on the homeowners' behavioral style. I then began the task of setting up teams intentionally. We would gather across the street from the damaged community at a Walgreens. I would look at the volunteers who showed up and do a quick evaluation of each person to try to determine whether they were a D, I, S, or C according to the DISC method. Then I would put teams together. This happened every day for months.

I made sure we had the Ds leading the charge, directing the team with the tasks that were needed at each homesite. I also picked at least one I style and elected them to knock on the door while the rest of the team stood back in the yard. They were so friendly as they introduced themselves, saying, "We are here for you, to assist you with whatever your need." These team members told the homeowners that we would help in every way, from hauling off debris to the nearest dumpster, ripping up soaked carpet and soggy floorboards, to removing drywall that had been saturated with water from the flood. We even had some homes that required our teams to crawl under the house to make sure all was structurally sound at the foundation level.

Once the homeowners agreed, I had one of my C volunteers present them with a release form to sign. Since Cs are all about correctness and protocol, they were super reliable in getting the forms signed and returned to the proper department. As a nonprofit organization, we had some liability releases that had to first be signed by the homeowners, releasing our teams from any liability in case something went south. We also found out that in disaster relief, when volunteers sign work orders, you can turn in those hours to FEMA and the state will receive funding for each volunteer hour recorded. This is one of those moments where the C type shines.

The S type volunteers were so amazing as they just did whatever was needed to help the families regain a sense of security. From sweeping the floors to listening to the concerns of the families impacted, the S was right there, fully engaged, compassionate, and loving. The strengths of every behavioral style were utilized in the middle of a crisis. It was so amazing to see the teams working so hard and heading home so full of life, knowing they were helping so many lives rebuild.

I made certain to reassure each one of our team members that our priority was loving people, however that translated to the homeowner and their family.

To ascertain this, I did a quick assessment of the personality types of homeowners. If they were an I, it meant that we would just listen as they talked through their concerns. Or maybe we laughed with them at their corny jokes because we realized that this was their way of processing the significant loss. We were able to help the I homeowners by presenting a list of things that were vital in creating a healthy, safe environment for their families. Most of these homeowners were more about talking it out than actually doing any work, so we had the teams doing the work for them.

If the homeowner was a D, we just went along with their plan and allowed them to direct our tasks. They knew exactly what they wanted us to help them accomplish, and we were quick to do so. Some were still in shock and came across as very bossy, but we knew this was just their way of processing what had just happened to them. We reassured them that they were strong and built for tough times. They were not only thankful for the extra hands and feet, but they were also grateful for the affirmation.

Our C homeowners were pretty easy to recognize because even in the midst of the storm damage, you could see the organization in their home. They had a place for their car keys, a spot for their bills. You could still see the order amid the chaos. We needed our teams to follow their protocol and ask, "Does this go here?" when attempting to put things back together. It was imperative that the C felt order was a priority and that our teams respected their homes.

Our S homeowners were more concerned about their family's feelings and personal items such as pictures, books—anything that held special memories. Their immediate concern was the safety of the home and all who were in it, whether family, friends, volunteers, or neighbors. They just wanted to make sure everyone in their community was safe.

As we spent several weeks and even months in this community, we gained a supreme trust equity with the homeowners and families. This became a favorable identity for our entire church. We found great favor when families were uncertain. They trusted our teams to come in and assist them without any strings attached. We didn't try to get them to go to our church. We just loved them with our actions.

Then, seven months after the flood, I received a frantic phone call.

"There's so much devastation everywhere, but one family especially needs help," said Mr. Knight, the dean of the Franklin Classical School. "That's why I'm calling you." (I'll call them the Newtons. This story is true, but, for obvious reasons, I've changed the family's identity. Their only son, Aaron, attended the same school where our son Isaac was enrolled. Because of the reputation of quality education, the school attracted students from all over the Nashville area.)

"What kind of help?" I asked. As a pastor's wife, I regularly heard cries for help.

"It's in Cottonwood," the dean said. He expressed concern for the family and their situation. "They don't own the house, which was flooded in May. Nothing has been done. It's left a terrible odor, and now the husband has walked out. Jean Newton and Aaron need help."

"What do they need?" I asked.

"Volunteers to show up and clean up the place. Just ask Jean what kind of help she needs. If you go there, you'll see the major damage."

During those months after the flood, absolutely nothing had been done to the Newton house. When Mr. Knight learned about the seriousness, he called me. He was worried about the effects of the damage to the health of those living there. They didn't own the house, and the owners had not responded.

With great concern, I immediately began to wonder if this family had been exposed to any type of mold, and I pondered how it may have affected their health. Urgency overwhelmed me as I began to make phone calls to assemble a team who would be able to brave this potentially hazardous situation. I remember my heart racing as I rushed to get over to this family. I remembered seeing them months prior as we served this neighborhood but thought for sure they had been helped by now. I was devastated and disappointed for them, but incredibly grateful that Mr. Knight had called me.

That same day, I organized a team of people from our church and went to the house. Just from opening the front door, the horrible odor overpowered us. It was a mixture of dampness and musty mold. I was immediately concerned for this sweet family. Jean took us to the top floor of the two-story home—the confined space where they had lived for seven months.

The breeze coming through the open windows helped, but the odor had permeated everything. It was now the beginning of winter, so it was very cold and drafty in the house. The reality that this family had lived here in these conditions broke my heart. They lived just a few miles away from my home. Our sons went to school together. How had she continued living here for so long?

"Why have you continued to live here?" I asked.

"We have nowhere else to go." She told us the story, often pausing to wipe her eyes. "My husband and I kept calling the owner of the property and never reached him."

Eventually, she learned that the elderly property owner had died—thus, the lack of response. His son, who inherited the property, finally answered her cries for help. "I'm not going to do anything," he said. "The place is a money pit." Then he added, "I'm going to put it on the market for sale as is."

The family agreed to buy the house, but, legally, they couldn't do anything to fix it until the sale closed.

In early December, someone came from the community of Cottonwood, checking on the remaining damage in their area. "This house is a health hazard," he said after he visited their home. "You need to clean this up."

"We don't own the house, and the owner won't let us do anything until—"

"I don't care what the owner says. You are endangering your lives by living in this mess."

He explained about the black mold, which is common after severe water damage from floods. It's actually greenish-black and usually has a bumpy appearance. The top layer is slimy to the touch.

"I don't want to alarm you," the man said, "but black mold is toxic to humans."

He listed symptoms such as breathing problems, headaches, fatigue, and nausea. "Brain fog is another serious effect and can result in mental problems."

"We have several of those symptoms," Jean said, "especially the breathing problems and—"

"Then do something about it, or move out."

Finally, they were able to buy the house but had no money to finish the remediation and renovation. As we toured the first floor of the home, we saw that some sort of remediation had started, but that it had just seemed to meet an abrupt end, leaving the efforts incomplete and the home full of dangerous exposure. We noticed several openings to the outside from walls that had been partially removed. By this time, the house had suffered severe damage from the flood and required much more than just the removal of the infested carpets, drywall, and furniture. I knew that our team members would be extremely helpful yet limited in our ability to complete the project. However, many of them had connections to general contractors who could assist Jean in rebuilding after we stepped in to remediate.

We discovered that the pressure from this experience was so intense that the husband just could not handle it anymore and left. This left Jean and her son to fend for themselves. They were too overwhelmed to know where to turn. Thank God this is where the dean of Franklin Classical was informed and stepped in.

I realized that Jean was literally living day by day, trying her best to take care of her son by creating a sense of comfort, and desperate for some sense of stability while dealing with the devastation of divorce. She was an S trying to find security but overwhelmed with shame, leaving her imprisoned in her own house.

When our team walked into the house, we saw several raccoons and squirrels having the time of their lives in the kitchen. They seemed to have found some sort of nourishment and were feeling convinced they would find more. Jean was using space heaters to ward out the cold air, but the draftiness was brisk inside.

Our team looked at everything. Carpets across all the floors needed to be ripped out and disposed of. We knew that would eliminate the worst of the stench.

"I feel stuck and helpless," Jean said to me as she wiped the tears from her eyes. "I can't do anything, and I didn't know where to turn."

"We'll do all we can," I assured her.

I took what I had learned in assisting the other homeowners in the Cottonwood neighborhood and arranged our volunteers according to their personality types. Each person was in the job that energized them. They quickly and joyfully completed the tasks to help the Newtons have a safe and clean house to call home.

The important point I want to make is that each of us felt joyful and fulfilled when we finished the renovation. We had treated our behavioral responses as gifts—talents from God.

Knowing our personality types, along with their strengths and areas of challenge, allows us to find our natural place in life. We won't waste time trying to be someone we were not made to be. As we learn and accept our unique and natural response in situations, we grow in self-understanding and deepen our relationships with others. And most of all, we grow closer to God, who loves us.

A Perfect Fit

"How did you get started with DISC?"

"Why is DISC so important to you?"

More than once, someone has asked those two questions. Here's my explanation.

Back in the mid-1990s, my husband, Danny, and I ministered at a youth conference in Louisiana. While there, the youth pastor's wife, Sherry, who has remained one of my closest friends, shared her positive experience from reading one of Tim LaHaye's books on identifying the four basic personality types.

His work was based on a theory by Hippocrates, the Greek physician and philosopher, and then modernized by LaHaye. The concept says that every person can be categorized as one of four different types. LaHaye's four personality types were identified as choleric, sanguine, phlegmatic, and melancholy.

My friend Sherry's eyes lit up as she explained that the study had revolutionized her personal life and marriage. Like me, she was married to what LaHaye called a choleric and the DISC system refers to as a D. She had often misunderstood his take-charge attitude. But her study enabled her to understand him more and also to recognize her own personality. This greatly influenced their marriage in a positive way as they began to understand the strengths of one another and not just end each day irritated at the way they made each other feel.

After listening to her, I became curious about my own personality and those around me. Over the next weeks, I devoured every book I found on the subject. As I gained insight, I began to realize the reasons I think the way I do, which then produced my behavior. That was something I hadn't previous considered.

As I continued to research, I learned why the people in my world behaved a certain way. It became clear to me that we're all wired differently. That concept helped me understand those who challenged me or doubted my insight, instead of my constantly fighting a feeling of insecurity. Through this research, I realized that their response was from seeing through a different lens—they responded that way because they perceived the world differently. That insight powerfully redirected my life. I began to approach every relationship in a distinct way. I determined to seek understanding before I expected to be understood. This empowered me to desire to recognize how others are wired so that I can effectively approach them with my words and actions. I will explain more in the chapters ahead.

The next and most important development happened when Danny and I attended a conference in the late nineties where we heard Dr. Sandy Kulkin teach on DISC. In many ways, he described the same theories and concepts of the four temperaments I had been studying. But for me, at least, it made it practical and exciting.

"Yes! Yes!" I wanted to shout. DISC made practical sense and, to me, seemed easier to digest. It was also much easier to explain to others.

Kulkin pointed out the four temperaments and offered a mnemonic device—a series of words that start with the same letter to help you remember.

D = Dominant, Direct, Driven

I = Inspiring, Innovative, Impulsive

S = Steady, Stable, Secure

C= Correct, Calculated, Conscientious

That brilliant speaker was also a consultant to various organizations. With the DISC model, he helped their human resources departments to hire the right people *based on their behavior.* This was revolutionary to me as I sat and listened to him pour out his wisdom and experience. The light switch flipped in my mind. We had always hired people based on a job description. We looked at the roles and responsibilities of a position and would see who we could squeeze into it based on their education and experience.

What if we were to turn that on its head? What would happen if we created a role and responsibility based on a person's natural wiring, the way they think and behave? Instead of fitting them into a role, why not formulate a role to fit them? My mind was rocked just thinking of this possibility.

Knowing how a person is wired is essential to giving them the right seat on the bus. That not only ensured the bus arrived at the correct destination, but the trip itself was also much more fun and enjoyable as everyone enjoyed their seat.

I was completely sold.

Although a bit shy, I introduced myself to Sandy Kulkin. He not only answered my questions with great clarity but also later became my mentor and coach. He encouraged me to go through his training. It wasn't as easy as an online course. It was twenty-four cassette tapes and an entire binder full of fill-in-the-blank worksheets. For those of you who remember, "rewind" and "fast forward" were the extent of navigation for cassettes. It was definitely an exercise in patience. In 2000, I graduated from his program—the DISC Assessment and Training—and have become a master coach for the DISC assessments through his organization, PeopleKeys.

DISC has tremendously influenced the way I do business. Hiring the right people for our business is an essential ingredient for successful results. Positioning the right person in the right role is vital for their sense of contribution and success. Or to use my bus model, the right person in the wrong seat is a pathway to failure.

When hiring a new employee, the first step is for them to take the assessment. Once I examine the results and see how they're wired, it's easier to determine whether the job is right for them.

I firmly believe that the question should not be, "Are you the right person for this job?" The question should be, "Is this the right job for you?" Forcing people to conform to a job description is a fast pass to a horrible roller-coaster ride.

Before jumping into the hiring process, a clear job description is basic. Without clarity of what employees are to expect, it's impossible to determine who's best suited for the job. If there are no clear expectations, how can you measure their capacity and celebrate their success?

To establish a healthy work environment, I encourage the creation of a job description based on the strengths of a person. Understanding a company's vision allows the big picture to drive the hiring instead of merely the need to fill a hole on their staff. Placing individuals in their sweet spot helps to secure their buy-in and commitment. When they get up in the morning, they're ready to rush to work. If they must press "snooze" ten times on their alarm clocks, it's time to rethink their responsibilities.

Positioning a person successfully is possible, especially when you can see their strengths through the assessment. Many times, businesses allow the urgent to overshadow the intentional. They are in such a rush to fill a position, they just hire the most educated or experienced person rather than look at how the person is wired and adjust the job description to fit their strengths. It's very sad when a person is placed in a position opposite their natural gifts. They end up deploring their job. Sometimes their responsibilities end up shifting as the needs of the business transition, and they find themselves in a seat that is foreign to their wiring. Are they introverts whose job transitioned them to function in front of the public? If so, that means they're so uncomfortable they want to pull the bedcovers over their head and hide.

Or maybe they gain energy from contributing ideas and strategies but they're locked inside a room behind a desk all day. They're ready to explode with no one to listen to their creative ideas.

This is true when recruiting or positioning volunteers as well. When I was leading a large church at three different locations, assimilating volunteers correctly became a full-time job. Just because a person signs up to help doesn't mean they can help wherever. In fact, I could write a book on how to lose a volunteer before you win them. People want to feel a sense of contribution. They must see that the investment of their time is making a difference. If you ask them to show up at a specific time, make sure you are there on time as well; and not only there to meet them, but to give them a clear expectation with simple directions of what they are to do so they can measure their efforts and walk away fulfilled enough to show up again. Nothing is more frustrating to a person who has taken time to show up and help than a lack of organization and direction.

The person who loves to talk needs to be at the front door, welcoming people into the church, the restaurant, or the business. Don't put them at the cash register counting the money. They'll get so distracted talking up a storm, it's likely they'll miscount and have to start counting all over again. Or worse, they miscount, and your entire business is off-balance.

You don't want to have to put all the fires out from misplacing people on your team. A quarterback might be able to knock people down, but you would never put him on the defensive line. And you sure don't want a linebacker playing wide receiver. There is a reason successful teams are successful. Coaches who recognize the sweet spot of their players and then create the plays that unleash their strengths win more games.

Understanding the strengths of a person truly helps to correctly position them in ministry, in business—even in their families.

Several years ago, I was asked to partner with other organizations in creating a nonprofit event to benefit women from our homeless community as well as those who were living in poverty, dependent on government aid to make ends meet.

Five women, all of us strong leaders who had influenced our city in different areas, agreed to host the event. For the occasion to be successful, we had to be willing to merge our different cultures and perceptions. That is, we had to understand each other to appreciate strengths and discover where our abilities fit into the various tasks. Each woman had her own style of leadership and behavior.

In the beginning, we ended up hitting several speed bumps. We would be progressing along, and then there would be a sudden change. The motive behind the change was always a good one. However, the change was so abrupt, it would throw the rest of us off. Slowly and unsuspectingly, disunity began to creep in. We realized if we were to be successful in this endeavor, we had to find a place of unity. This did not come easily; we had to choose to give each other grace. This was the first time we had all worked together. We were not only merging business cultures, but we were also learning how to work together with all four different behavioral styles. Because our goal was to value and love women who were struggling with self-worth, we pressed through our differences and worked together.

More than twelve hundred women participated in the two-day event. We had partnered with local businesses, and collected clothing, personal items, and toiletries which we bagged for the women to freely take. We provided hot meals, showers, and physical checkups such as dental, blood pressure, and mammograms. Salon stylists offered hair care and new hairdos to make the women feel beautiful. Although imperfect, the venture was definitely successful and productive for the women who participated.

We five leaders learned a lot about each other, and over the years we've become close friends. And yet, each of us is different. We grew in our understanding of our differences so we could best work with each other.

Understand Yourself, Understand Others

"Why should I learn about DISC?" That question comes regularly, and I never tire of answering it.

My first response is that it is a form of *self*-awareness as well as *other*-awareness. Too often people struggle as they try to understand others—a good thing—but they try to do it without first knowing themselves. Or they focus totally on self-knowledge and don't reach out to understand others.

To be emotionally healthy and to grow, we need both to grasp who we are and to use that understanding to enable us to understand others—especially those we consider different or have difficulty liking. We all have people in our lives who we would prefer not to invite out for coffee. I'm not saying you should feel obligated to spend time with these people. I am suggesting that you consider being open to understand them better. This will only serve to increase your own capacity to relate to people. Understanding their behavior does not necessarily mean you approve of it. It just means you have positioned yourself with greater potential to see success when you choose to take the time and make the effort to understand them. Understanding empowers action. My personal motto is, "Clarity is power." To me, this means the clearer I can see, the more power I possess to accurately move forward. Oftentimes we jump to conclusions and then end up missing the point.

If we think we are about to be rejected, we will spend our energy proving our importance by bragging on our accomplishments, dropping names, and jockeying for the center of attention. One comment of affirmation from someone else will disarm the verbal army of self-compliments that often serve to cloak our fear of rejection. Knowing this about ourselves will assist us in recognizing it in others and direct our conversation accordingly.

Frequently, those who seek security will emotionally check out at the first sign of insecurity or change. They turn their facial expression on autopilot while silently formulating their strategy to justify their comfort and refusal to cooperate. Consistent assurance of peace and harmony will lift the burden of the already imagined pain of change, and you will see their genuine facial expression once again.

Critical eyes often self-criticize. They also filter the words of others through a personal criticism filter. Their need for correctness comes complete with strong boundaries that must only be crossed with valid credentials such as permission and fact-backed information. Preparedness and appreciation for their calculations will help soften the tone of conversation and leave you feeling very well-informed to make the best decision. Understanding that they hear through a filter of criticism will empower a well-thought-out response and hopefully diffuse a potential bomb.

This is a powerful concept when applied to relationships of any kind. *We must first seek to understand before seeking to be understood.*

In my attempt to deepen my knowledge of DISC, I read about the elevator parable, and I like to share it with others.

Think of a small elevator intended to hold only four people and that number already fills the space. Just as the door starts to close, an extremely large woman cries out, "Hold the door," and rushes to get inside. A petite grandmother steps out and blocks the door from closing. "Come on, we can squeeze in one more person." She then proceeds to tell this new passenger how glad she is that she made it onto the elevator and to share how her day has been so far, barely taking a breath in between sentences. The other three automatically bunch a little closer.

Dom, a task-oriented man, doesn't say anything, but he frowns and thinks, *I'm in a hurry. She could have waited for the next elevator instead of holding us back.* The frustration escaping his mind is seen through the very loud patting of his foot and several intense glances at his watch.

Ernie, a middle-aged gate agent for an airline, says nothing but smiles and shrugs at the woman who nudges into the already crowded space. He is silently happy to help her get to where she needs to be and questions the inconsiderate foot tapping of his fellow passenger.

Connie, the fourth occupant, looks for the occupancy sign, wondering if they've exceeded the weight limit. *If we're overweight,* she thinks, *the elevator might refuse to move.* Just as she begins to get anxious, the elevator closes and up they go.

That simple illustration is a quick view of the various personalities identified as D, I, S, C. By their behavior, they self-reveal.

Let's examine them briefly. I'll provide more details in later chapters.

The enthusiastic grandmother who held the door is obviously people oriented, emotional, and demonstrative. On the DISC chart, we call her an I. Her motto is, "The more the merrier." She loves life and is full of words.

Dom, the task-oriented man, we call a D. Think of the word *dominant*—this is a descriptive word and not a judgment. People like Dom tend to be extroverted, optimistic, direct. They are doers. Coworkers would say, "Dom gets the job done." They would also say, "He sometimes comes across as cold and indifferent." In the elevator, Dom is most likely in a rush to make a life-altering presentation that will bring great increase to a listening group of people.

Ernie, the gate agent, fits under S. He's a peacemaker, sympathetic, quiet, steady, and easygoing. He is not at all inconvenienced by the addition of this person and is most likely contemplating and guessing where this new passenger is headed and why.

Connie, the final occupant, represents C because she's introverted, a thinker, and competent but cautious. She plays by the rules. After all, they are there for a reason.

You might relate your normal behavior with one of the characters in my illustration. Or you may have said, "I see a little of myself in all of them."

Beware of labels. DISC is not a label maker but a way to assess who you are and how you come across to others. For example, I'm female, tall, and blonde. Those are three descriptive words, but I'm not limited to those characteristics. They don't tell you who I am.

Too many use labels or terms to define people. They only access resources like DISC to put people in a box and ship then off to Stereotype Springs. Instead, they need to try to see the information as a tool to learn more about themselves and others. DISC, when used properly, helps achieve that double purpose, to assess who you are and how you are perceived.

DISC is most popular among human resources departments, where people work who do the hiring for a business or organization. That seems wise to me because DISC is based on the way applicants respond to situations.

DISC also offers hope in its assessment, saying, "Once you know who are, you can modify your behavior." Immediately I think of the words of God through the prophet Jeremiah. At least three times, God pleads, "Amend your ways and your doings." (See Jeremiah 7:3, 5; 26:13 NKJV.) Why would God *command* the Israelites to change if it were impossible?

The approach in this book is to *know yourself*. And once you know who you are, you can go on to understand others. As you change, you can, in your behavioral style, encourage others to modify their actions as well.

Let's be specific. Why is knowing and understanding personality styles important? I have four answers.

Understanding personality styles helps you

▸ become a better communicator. It's difficult to get along with people you don't understand. You can easily misinterpret actions or words and get frustrated. Once you understand different personality styles, you find the key to unlock better communication.

▸ resolve or prevent conflicts. When you understand *why* someone did or said something, you will be less likely to react negatively. An awareness of another's underlying motivations can allow you to diffuse problems before they even start.

▸ appreciate the differences in others. You know that all people are unique, but sometimes you get frustrated with those who don't quite fit your communication style. Learning about styles gives you the ability to appreciate the differences.

▸ gain credibility and positively influence others. By knowing how to blend or adapt with another's style, you can immediately gain credibility and influence.

Another way of saying this is that I want people to learn to *be* in a room. That means they recognize others in that place. The tendency is to see the people who are like you and ignore others. For example, Ds and Is tend to see those like themselves—visibly active, assertive, and the centers of the action. The introverted C and S are often hiding in a corner or speaking to only a limited group.

My goal is to avoid that segregation and help you enrich yourself and others by getting to know the people who are different. In doing so, you learn to appreciate them for who they are. And if you truly think about it and practice reaching out to those who tend to be unlike yourself, two positive things occur.

First, you're enriched by them. You can learn from them. Their perspectives can cause you to rethink your actions and attitudes; you can receive new insights by listening and interacting with others. You can expand your circle when you include different facets of thinking. Much like a diamond, the more facets, the greater the value.

Second, you stand up against isolation by entering into community with others. Individuality is a threat when it is the center of motivation. The predator knows the best time to strike is when the prey is alone and isolated from the others. Isolation means there is no one to warn against the enemy and no one to come alongside and defend and protect. Individuality is powerful when combined with others. It is vital to be true to who you are yet not remain alone. We are meant to live and work and play with others. John Donne said it best in one of his sermons:

"No man is an island, entire of itself; every man is a piece of the continent, a part of the main. If a clod be washed away by the sea, Europe is the less, as well as if a promontory were, as well as if a manor of thy friend's or of thine own were: any man's death diminishes me, because I am involved in mankind, and therefore never send to know for whom the bell tolls; it tolls for thee."

CHAPTER FOUR

What Is DISC?

DISC is an acronym introduced by American psychologist Dr. William M. Marston in the late 1920s. He developed a personality model based on the ideas of four primary behavioral traits that he referred to as DISC for Dominance, Influence, Steadiness, and Compliance.

DISC, which has been refined in recent years, was established as a *nonjudgmental tool* to enable individuals to understand behavioral differences—their own and others. An important ingredient is that all four types are acceptable and valued. There is no good or bad, no better or worse, only differences.

As we take this journey through DISC, I want to point out you're probably a blend of more than one style. Those whose behavior is predominantly one way, we call *High*, such as High S. I myself am a combination of SIC. This means that on the assessment my S was the highest yet my I and C were included in the results. I'll explain, but first, let's look at some simple ways to identify some of the traits that reveal behavior.

You reveal who you are by your mannerisms; your behavioral style follows the adage, "Your actions speak louder than your words." You could say this helps determine how you are wired.

For example, two individuals come down the grocery aisle toward you. One moves quickly, nods or smiles at you, and keeps going. The slower person probably won't look directly at you or acknowledge your presence. Both are learned forms of behavior, and you can learn a great deal about their types by observing how they act.

Someone said, "If you want to know how a person thinks, observe the way they stand or their response when someone talks to them." Observing others is a skill most people can learn. That's a major reason for writing this book—to empower you to understand others.

Effective communication depends on reading others correctly. Think about this: if I can understand you and you can understand me, the obvious result is that we can work together more effectively. Understanding behavioral style and the way we are wired helps to improve your personal and working relationships with others. It will also increase your awareness of how you respond to conflict. Along with this you can learn about your stresses and motivation.

DISC focuses on a positive approach. This isn't to enable you to concentrate on the weaknesses of others, but to see their strengths and appreciate who they are. I hope your observations will remain flexible as you remind yourself that every individual is a unique blend.

From this book, I hope you'll learn to perceive *yourself* in a favorable light—accepting and appreciating your special uniqueness. Second, I hope you'll accept other perceptions and values as favorable, especially when they disagree with yours.

Here I'll remind you of the four types of behavioral styles comprising DISC, along with the common mnemonic device of each to help you recall them. Please note, this is not describing *personality types*. The DISC model is a *behavioral style* model.

▸ D stands for Dominant, Direct, and Driven. This refers to about 3 percent of people.

▸ I refers to Inspiring, Innovative, and Impulsive. About 11 percent of the population fits this category.

▸ S indicates Steady, Stable, and Secure, and that is about 69 percent, which is obviously the largest group.

▸ C stands for Correct, Calculated, and Conscientious, and makes up about 17 percent of people.

Each of the four forms of behavior surface in various situations. You don't always give the same type of response. Differing situations call for differing behavior. This doesn't mean, however, that we display all four styles. Most people favor one or two, with perhaps a hint of a third behavioral style as seen in a DISC assessment.

To better empower you, I've included in this chapter a simple version of the DISC assessment. It is very important that you first decide which environment you would like to put yourself in as you answer the questions. For example, if you decide that you would like to assess your behavior at home, answer the questions as if you were in your living room. Your answers will reflect your home behavior. It could answer the question your spouse has been asking, "Why can't you just talk to me?" Or maybe help you understand that talking through everything is very important to you, but maybe your child needs time to process and think before they talk it out.

For some, behavior at home is somewhat different than behavior at work. Earlier I shared with you that my behavioral style is SIC. This was my assessment in my work environment. I took the assessment as if I were sitting at my desk in my office. My answers to the questions were reflective of my working behavior. At work I am more of a coach, counselor, teacher, listener. I can take the lead role if needed, but I prefer to help others find their sweet spot and assist them with their tasks. This is the High S. My I loves to stop by each person's office on my way to mine to simply say hello; not necessarily interrupt them, but acknowledge their presence and appreciate them. I have just enough C in me to notice if a light bulb is out or if there is a stain on the carpet. But I'm not the best to proofread because the S in me automatically sees what should be there, so my brain just fixes whatever is misspelled while leaving the actual misspelling on the paper.

Due to my SIC combination, when taking the assessment in my home environment my C becomes more dominant. Perhaps it's because I've been married for thirty years and have five children, four of whom are married, and eight grandchildren. And believe me, this is just the beginning.

The more my family grew, the more my inner C rose. Somewhere along the journey, I decided I could no longer waste precious time looking for my lost keys, the TV remote, or my cell phone. In fact, ask any of my children—if they come to the house and lay their keys down on the counter or coffee table, I sweep in with my Wonder Woman cape, swoop up those keys just before they get kidnapped by one of the tiny, little-fingered munchkins, and hang them safely on the key holder.

Brilliant! you might say. Well thank you, but this brilliance came at the one-time cost of a certain experience where a sneaky toddler accidentally dropped the keys of their unsuspecting auntie into their diaper bag. This little stunt instigated an all-hands-on-deck investigation throughout the house, elevating blood pressures and summoning lots of tears for hours. The investigation ended in a very sorrowful phone call from the mother of the little thief.

This key holder cost about $9.99 yet has saved thousands of wasted hours on search campaigns.

As you can see, determining in which environment to take the assessment is vital to understanding your behavior in that environment. Some people are the same both at home and work, yet others like me, might experience a bit of a difference.

Each of the questions has four answers. You are to rate each answer with the numbers 1-4; 4 is the most representative of you, and 1 is the least. A few questions may seem to be a tie, where the answers are just too much alike to select which is most like you. This is where you call a lifeline to help you select the answer that best describes you. Just make sure the person you reach out to for help truly knows you enough to advise you. Each one of your answers affects the outcome.

You are just about ready to take your simple assessment. There's just one more thing. To prevent the inevitable mind monster—overthinking—to hijack your results, set a timer. Grab your cell phone or some type of timer and give yourself seven minutes. This is just enough time to complete the assessment without too much time to second-guess yourself.

Okay, here's a quick recap, before you take this assessment:

1. Determine your environment (work or home).

2. Read each phrase horizontally and rate them as follows: 1 as the least like you, 2 as less like you, 3 as somewhat like you, and 4 as the most like you.

For example:

Adventurous, Risk-taker 2	Trusting, Believing in others 4	Easygoing, Agreeable 3	Tolerant, Respectful 1

3. Set a timer for seven minutes, and don't overthink it. Ready? Here you go:

DISC Assessment

Adventurous, Risk-taker	Trusting, Believing in others	Easygoing, Agreeable	Tolerant, Respectful
Optimistic, Visionary	Center of Attention, Sociable	Peacemaker, Helper	Soft-spoken, Reserved
Goal Setter	Cheerleader	Team Player	Strives for Perfection
Determined	Talkative	Balanced	Rule Follower
Fighter	Over-promises	Resists Change	Withdraws under pressure
A good delegator	A good encourager	A good listener	A good analyzer
Results matter	Make it fun	Do it together	Accuracy matters

Challenge rules	Rules are boring	Rules make it safe	Rules make it fair	
Want authority	Want opportunity	Want peace	Want clear directions	
I will lead them	I will persuade them	I will follow through	I will get the facts	
Take Charge	Enthusiastic, Outgoing	Consistent, Predictable	Cautious, Careful	
Competitive	Optimistic, Positive	Think of others first	Logical, Systematic	
D	I	S	C	=120

Once you've rated your answers horizontally, add them up vertically, putting your score beside the D, I, S, C. All your numbers together horizontally should add up to 120. If this is not the case, you need to recalculate. Whichever letter has the highest score reflects your dominant behavioral style.

Well, how did you do? It wasn't that difficult, was it? Please understand, this is a simple version used to identify your dominant behavioral style. And now that you have identified it, the rest of this book will empower you at a whole new level. It will also empower you to operate in your strengths.

We have a saying, "Go where you're celebrated, not where you're tolerated." By finding your behavioral style, you can do exactly that. You can learn to put yourself in environments that flow with your natural strengths. That's first—figure out who you are and where you function best. When you're contented and at peace, you know you're where you belong. Try to avoid those situations for which you're not naturally bent. You'll know these by the lack of peace that accompanies them.

As you go through this book with me, I'll guide you to ponder your natural limitations—and we all have them. Even in such situations, you can usually find opportunities to grow. And you'll need to face those issues and realign your ability. If you're willing to face those limitations by acknowledging and correcting them, you'll be empowered to press on and to grow.

Please notice, I don't call them *weaknesses*. That's a judgmental call, as if something is wrong with you. That's not the point of DISC. My goal and that of the program is to assist you to accept yourself *as you are* and guide you to adapt your actions and attitudes to become more effective in your relationships.

To become more effective is another way of saying to empower you to live a successful and contented life.

CHAPTER FIVE

Dominant D

Have you ever met someone who just seemed to have it all together? Someone who was the best at *everything*? Not only have I met someone like this, I married this person. My husband Danny is amazing. So much so that people actually referred to him as "the total package." Talk about intimidating. Try being married to "the total package." Danny is an incredible singer, songwriter, producer. He is also one of the most effective public communicators I've ever heard. And in my line of work, I've heard plenty.

When we first got married, I was überinsecure. Constantly criticizing myself and comparing myself with ghosts of relationships past. Why I compared myself with others who were no longer even around is just a mystery—yet I did.

In 1990, when Danny and I got married, we traveled all over the world, mostly to churches and conferences. He would sing and speak. He was on numerous television broadcasts as well as on radio. See what I mean, the total package? He was in this particular industry for a decade before we were married, so he had all kinds of experience.

I'll never forget the first time I was asked to cohost a television program with him. It was awful! Have you ever heard of the Cindy Brady Syndrome? Well, I may have just made it up. There was an episode on *The Brady Bunch* where the Bradys were all on a television show together. The youngest daughter, Cindy, completely overwhelmed by the cameras and lights, froze up and went into a zombie stare. Yep, that was me. The trophy wife of the total package on her television debut, frozen in front of millions of viewers. My husband, Prince Charming for real, answered every question like a pro. Needless to say, I had even more insecurity to overcome. You'll be happy to know that I did indeed overcome and buried the zombie once and for all.

Before I studied DISC, even though I loved my husband, I often had trouble understanding him. I so admired the way he always seemed to know exactly what he wanted. He rarely struggled to make a decision. And he walked in such great confidence. All great attributes, especially for the CEO of our organization; yet, at times, he seemed reactive instead of responsive. He would talk off the top of his head instead of thinking through his decision. Danny is an external processor. He *talks through* things. I am an internal processor. I *think through* things. To him, my silence was the death sentence to his ideas. To me, my silence was those internal steps I was taking to get us from here to there, "there" being the success of his idea.

By the time I would reach the destination in my mind, carefully plotting the path on how to get there safely, he would change course and set a new destination. This caused me to eventually learn that I needed to wait until he had talked it all the way through, considered options, looked at it from several angles, and talked through each angle. Then, before starting my internal journey to the destination, I'd ask, "Are you certain this is what you want to do?" Once I got his confirmation, I would then have the necessary credentials to begin the journey.

When I discovered that this is just how Danny is wired, it truly brought me peace. I used to think he was changing his mind all the time just to get on my nerves. But no, he is a risk-taker, an adventurer. He's on the *Starship Enterprise,* boldly going where no man has gone before. He's exciting and mysterious. He loves to challenge the norm. In fact, I used to think he was challenging me. I took it personally and would find myself totally shutting down. After studying the DISC, I discovered that he was just challenging the status quo of life. He is not content to be like everyone else or do what everyone else does. He didn't mind drawing attention to himself; he knew exactly what to do with it. He understood that people often need someone to lead them. He knew he could lead them to their purpose or at least introduce them to the One who gave them their purpose.

I was just so insecure. I thought he was somehow trying to turn me into himself. My lack of self-confidence had me on a wild-goose chase trying to figure out what exactly he was "really" trying to say or what did he "really" mean. Because I spoke in insinuations, I automatically assumed that he did too. Several heart-to-heart conversations later, it finally connected that he was not trying to turn me into himself. Why would he do that? He fell in love with me. The me he fell in love with was nothing like him. In fact, what good would it be for either of us to be exactly the same? One of my mentors says, "If two of you are exactly alike, one of you is unnecessary." The fact that we are exact opposites is an asset; it's a huge benefit. I had to shift my paradigm from seeing this as a problem. It was not a problem at all, it was a huge blessing. Danny is just wired differently; he is a D.

Throughout our marriage, I have grown significantly and learned how to access Danny's strengths. He has truly helped me grow beyond my insecurities and understand that confidence is not cockiness. And I have had plenty of opportunities to share my strengths and assist Danny in his areas of growth. He would also be super quick to make changes, even if they seemed unnecessary to me. His confidence at times would drift into strong opinions that would often shut me down. He's definitely a D. When I was able to determine his style, we greatly improved our level of communication.

For example, Danny is a delegator. He's a great visionary and also practical. Those two qualities don't always go together.

With Danny, his frequently assigning tasks to others seemed like dumping—which shows I didn't understand this part of him. Finally, I pulled him aside and said, "Whether you mean it that way or not, there's a perception that you just drop tasks on others because you don't want to do them."

The shock on his face made me realize he had no idea that anyone saw him that way.

After becoming familiar with DISC, I was able to say it more diplomatically. "You need to repackage the way you allocate jobs for others."

At first, he didn't seem to understand what I was implying. Or, more likely, being what we call a High D, he didn't take criticism easily and became defensive. Despite that, he knew I loved him and wanted the best for him, so he continued listening.

"You're giving them more and more things to do—"

"What's wrong with that?"

"What's wrong is that you *assign* them work instead of first asking them and getting them to buy into your ideas."

The look on Danny's face made me realize he had heard me.

"One more thing. You delegate and overload them—and you forget they're volunteers—working free as part of their service to God. They don't have the same vision or level of commitment that, as the leader and visionary, you do."

Danny nodded and finally said, "Repackage, huh? How do I repackage?"

"Enable them to see each task as an opportunity for service—for ministry—because they want to contribute and advance the Kingdom of God. Almost every time, you have the ability to select the right person to get the tasks completed. That's a gift. But now you need to learn to use the right approach."

I know you have heard it said, "It's not what you say it, it's how you say it." Well, let me introduce you to a little formula I like to call "packaging." It's not just how you say it, it's how they hear it. You see, when you understand how a person is wired, you will also understand the value of packaging what you are saying in a way that the listener can hear and understand. Most people focus on how they say it but fail to think about how it's being heard. This could be why miscommunication wins. Fifty percent of successful communication is how you speak; the other 50 percent is how they hear. Danny was excellent at saying the right things, but he needed to recognize that hearing the right thing was just as valuable. When you consider how a person might hear, you can reconsider how you can say it better.

We actually have this exercise we do at the end of any deep or important conversation. Whether it's between us, our children, employees, or anyone, we end the conversation with this very important question: "What did you hear me say?" This question seems so simple, right? When we first began this exercise, we were often shocked at the responses, and you would not believe the answers we've heard throughout the years. In fact, it's proof that eye contact, head nodding, and even a quiet yes in no way assures that the listener is actually hearing what is being said. It's absolutely amazing how words can leave one set of lips, soar through the air, land on two ears, slide into the brain for sorting, and end up completely misinterpreted as it comes out the listener's mouth. So many opportunities for distraction abound nowadays, it's a miracle anyone actually hears and understands what's being said.

Let me encourage you to begin packaging your words more effectively and ending any vital conversation with this same question, "What did you hear me say?" Just remember to give grace upon hearing the answer.

Because Danny understood that the tasks he was handing out were to help in the ministry of reaching the hurting and lost, he assumed others did as well. Yet as I observed his leadership with others—and to me as his wife—I sometimes felt he was delegating something he didn't want to do or to be bothered with. At the same time, he saw it as expressing his trust in us to help him get the jobs done.

His self-sufficiency bothered me—probably because I lacked that quality. In my pre-DISC days, he came across as cold and unsympathetic. Only later did I grasp that, as a D, his unconscious motive was to make things right.

One of the first things I learned from my course at the Institute of Motivational Living was that Danny fit the profile of what we call a High D. These people are decisive, optimistic, and courageous. People like Danny aren't afraid to take risks. Consequently, he and those like him become strong leaders. Unlike many others, they grasp the whole picture and already intuitively know the dangers and pitfalls. Because they get it, they naturally assume others do as well.

At home, a D parent can wonderfully motivate the family to keep going, just as they can in the business world. They stay on top of things and have a vital need to see that things are done correctly.

"With a father like you, Danny, there's not a lot of laziness around the house," I once said. "You're organized, and you keep the household on schedule."

My mother, a High D, held the most amazing jobs over the years. She is a brilliant go-getter and very successful at everything she puts her mind to. When we lived in California in the early 1970s, my mom worked for NBC. She worked on *The Tonight Show* with Johnny Carson, organized benefits and events, hosted Elvis Presley, and was the script censor for two brand-new shows: *Bonanza* and *Star Trek*. I love hearing her share stories of how the network critics predicted that *Star Trek* would never last. "No one is into science fiction," they told Mom. Well, *Star Trek* certainly outlasted their critics.

Growing up, my mom left us lists. After school I would come home to a list of chores, one of which was to put the casserole that had spent the day defrosting into the oven so that by the time she and Dad returned home from work, we could sit down and have dinner together. My mom was so organized. My younger sister and I would spend most Saturdays following our list of chores along with my dad and his "honey-do" list, cleaning the house while Mom spent hours in the kitchen making casseroles. She would freeze them so we could make them for dinner and stay on budget. Setting aside this one day a week to clean and prepare for the upcoming week taught me so many valuable lessons. We were a team. We each had our responsibilities and, once completed, we each had privileges. My mother taught me that privilege and responsibility go hand in hand. You can't have one without the other without consequences. All responsibility and no privilege would burn you out. All privilege and no responsibility would consume you and burn you up. It was important to find balance. After a long day of cleaning, we would go out for ice cream or go bowling. I grew up learning how to balance fun and obligations.

Another thing I realized in being married to Danny and working with other D styles is that they yearn for positions of authority. That's part of their personality DNA. Along with that authority, they want freedom to do things their way. And being ambitious, they also seek opportunities for advancement.

As my understanding increased, I had to keep in mind that Danny, like other Ds, is goal oriented and thrives on opposition. It causes him to work harder. Or another way to say it is the opposition causes the D style to excel. Disagreeing with them forces out the better part of their personalities and behavioral style.

In the previous chapter I used three words to define the D: Dominant, Direct, Driven. In my experience, I'd add the word *debate*.

One of their best qualities is they take personal responsibility for their actions and believe they have made the best possible decision. Their blind spot is that they may be correct but not always popular with others. You see, not everything about a D—as well as the other styles—is a positive. Rather than label a characteristic as negative or as a weakness, I refer to it as *a limitation versus a strength*. For all the fine qualities in each type, people don't always see the downside. In fact, when I read back assessments to clients, at least 80 percent of them are shocked when I point out the limitations. Their response is often along the lines of, "Really? I didn't know that. Are you sure?"

I silently remind myself that their response is not an argument but part of their struggle to integrate what the assessment indicates.

As I list the traits of their style, I explain that they're not locked into that mode of behavior; it means they haven't figured out how to repackage. In my experience, only about 30 percent clearly recognize themselves. Most of the time, it's a big surprise. When I've done coaching sessions with Ds and pointed out their directness, they seemed shocked.

"I'm just frank and straightforward," one woman said defensively.

I smiled but kept silent.

"You mean—?" She was perceptive enough to hear her own words. "I never thought being frank had that effect on others."

Like many D types, she didn't perceive that her directness was coming across as rude or critical. She had internalized it as being truthful or honest. As we talked, she said, "It's important for the people I deal with to be correct. Too often, they're just wrong. I thought I was being helpful in setting them straight."

Although I didn't say it to her, I thought, *And you wonder why you don't have a lot of friends.*

In her defense, her desire to assist others in being the best they can be is an admirable trait, but the truth of the matter is, most people do not care how much you know until they know how much you care.

This motto of "setting people straight" often left her doing the work alone, leaving her overwhelmed and overstressed, adding to her intensity. It can become a never-ending cycle, producing loneliness and depression. She even admitted to the constant feeling of being misunderstood. She shed genuine tears upon this reality. My compassion was thoroughly engaged.

For her own sanity, it was vital to recognize that others took her directness as bossiness and sometimes bullying. I had to help her see how she could direct others from a posture of appreciation and "repackage" to make others feel valued instead of leaving them feeling belittled by her superiority.

If You Are a D

If you're a High D, one potential significant downside is that you don't think you need a lot of friends. Why would you? You pride yourself on being productive (and you probably are). You deeply care for the few true friends you have, but there is always an underlying sense that they are most likely using you for something.

In your mind, production is more important than people. It's just the way you are wired. You don't care who gets it done, or even how it gets done, you just want it done immediately. This can be a positive when the timelines are realistic. Pushing things through is a huge strength of a D. Encouraging people to rise above their limitations and step out and take the risk can be very rewarding. Just be aware that your drive is unique to you and others might feel more pushed than led.

This is why it is so easy for Ds to become workaholics. The pride in the completion of one project drives you to start another and then another. It's rare that you naturally know when to push away from your desk. The drive to do more fills your tank with a sense of self-gratification. Unfortunately, when being driven becomes more important than being with those you love, you're paying too high a price. That's part of what we mean when we say you are driven. The task becomes so important, you probably don't know how to unplug or relax.

Because of your workaholic nature, you remain so busy that you say you don't have time to spend with your family. Consequently, you miss out on many intimate and rewarding times.

Caution to the D: don't become so driven that you end up alone for the entire journey of life. You can find the balance between people and production. Both are a necessary component of a joyful and fulfilled life. Make your to-do list but include "spending quality time with loved ones" as a task, and you will reprogram your paradigm of family time into productive time.

At your worst, you come across as sarcastic or cruel, especially when you're joking. Because you are allergic to imperfection, you often place unrealistic expectations on yourself and others. Be cautious how you kid around. What you consider humorous could be perceived as severe criticism masquerading as just having fun.

Thousands of dollars have been spent in therapy sessions as professional listeners find their ears filled with different versions of the same story, the story of being neglected or never being good enough. "My dad never had time for me." "My mom always said I was lazy and would never amount to anything." "They always said I was too fat to fit in."

You name it, I've heard it. The words of a parent are the most significant and influential in a child's life. When those words are received as hurtful, the child will go to any cost to get approval and affirmation. If they don't receive positive affirmation, they will run the other way. After all, negative attention is still attention. Many teens find themselves serving up revenge to repay their parents for the pain they feel they have caused. Whether intentional or not, or even accurate, it's real to them. If you are a D parent, add to your to-do list "unconditional affirmation of those I love." Your words carry more weight than you realize. To be honest, I would advise you to delete sarcasm from your vocabulary altogether and find another hobby. It's not worth the few shallow giggles. It does more harm than good.

In family issues or a close friendship, you tend to dominate, whether it's a conversation, a family game night, or planning a summer vacation. Try to let others share their ideas. Try accepting someone else's vacation plans before enforcing your own. If you really want to grow and reveal your maturity, let others win. I know, I know, this sounds impossible. But I believe in you. You can do it. Just once, try to let someone else feel the air beneath their wings that comes from winning the game. Let them feel the dryness of their teeth as the ginormous smile of pride overtakes their face. You've felt it so many times, you don't even realize your upper lip gets stuck and you look like Cindy-Lou Who from Dr. Seuss's *How the Grinch Stole Christmas!* Hand over the "Get of Jail Free" card, and let others feel the freedom of actually playing the game. You might be surprised how undramatic losing a game of Clue really is.

Especially if you're a High D, you struggle with saying, "I'm sorry," or "Please forgive me." Instead, you typically find a reason why it's not your fault. An enlightened High D friend once said, "I used to shoot myself in the foot and then blame someone else for giving me the gun." Be careful how you present yourself to others. It's okay to be right, but if nobody in the room follows, then you're right—but all by yourself.

High Ds have little tolerance for mistakes. Because of your ability to focus on the whole picture, you're not good with details and tend to avoid the little things. With small talk you become bored and your responses may come across as brusque or rude.

Because you are looking for the bottom line, you can come across as impatient and insensitive. Fast-forwarding the conversation may save time, but it will cost you in respect. Your attention is a gift. Your eye contact says you value all the work put into this project. Your patience in waiting your turn is a form of honor. But this can all be undone by your body language telling another to, "Just get to the point already." And the rolling of the eyes is like a sniper on the rooftop of dreams. Be mindful of your facial expressions. Your body language often speaks louder than your words.

Take a deep breath and listen all the way to the end. Don't interrupt when you think you've heard the point. Finishing sentences for others only works for toddlers and foreign language speakers who are actually relieved to hear that you understand them. If you wait until they arrive at a period to respond instead of hijacking the conversation the moment they inhale, you might truly hear what they intend to say. Your incorrect assumption often causes the communicator to lose hope and decide to quit altogether. Their silence is not necessarily a choice. Perhaps your constant interruption has depleted their energy and their silence is the only way to recharge. Even if you knew what they were going to say, let them say it.

These are some limitations a D should pay attention to. If you have a great idea that you want to be able to lead, you have to forecast it in such a way that everyone wants to rally behind you. You don't want to forecast it in such a way that you actually push people away from you. Do that through the way you communicate, the way that you package it.

Interacting with a D Style

▸ Speak to the point. Be as direct as they are. I used to hear people say, "Stand up, speak up, and shut up." Good advice. Don't prolong discussions.

▸ Be prepared for strong rebuttal. A typical D enjoys challenge and may fiercely refuse to admit to making errors of judgment.

- Ask, "If I do this, exactly what are your expectations of me?"

- In any kind of team meeting where they're not in charge, they want to be asked. They respond glowingly to requests such as, "Would you mind functioning as the hostess?"

- Remind yourself that what may come across as being bossy or overwhelming isn't a personal attack.

- Don't deprive them of earned recognition. If you appreciate what they've done, tell them. They yearn for recognition for the effort they invest in their professional and private lives.

- Honor their need for autonomy.

- Show them you're competent, self-sufficient, and you can handle the task.

- Ask them to clarify the expectations for the task they've assigned you.

- Don't expect a lot of social interaction.

- Don't expect an apology. Words such as "I was wrong" aren't in the vocabulary box.

- Recognize their leadership traits and affirm them for their courage to take risks.

The world would be a different place without High Ds. In fact, think about it: if Christopher Columbus didn't have an adventurous spirit, students all over the world might be referring to a flat, pizza-style rendition of the world instead of the round multi-colored globe we use today. Risk-takers become inventors who save the planet, develop innovative technology, and expedite progress. They challenge theories, defend honor, and rush into dangerous situations rescuing those in need.

CHAPTER SIX

Inspiring I

I'll call her Sarah, although the story is true. She worked for a company specializing in technology development. She didn't have a college degree in engineering, but she definitely had grown to master the art of human interaction. She was very energetic and lit up the room as soon as she walked in. She was genius at making people feel valued and seemed to keep her audience captivated by her quick wit and charm.

"Even if they paid Sarah just to make others feel better," the office manager once said, "it would be worth the money." No matter how bad anyone felt, Sarah's effortless vitality and genuine interest in others pulled them right out of their depression or sadness. The whole team's self-value and self-appreciation levels went up with Sarah being around. But, like every other personality type, Sarah had her limitations. Sarah had difficulty overpromising and underdelivering. She always meant well. Her idealistic passion to help others often left her stranded somewhere between the beginning of a project and the finish line. Overwhelmed with the boredom of unfinished business, she would reignite her energy by starting something new. Or better yet, she would volunteer to help someone else with something that sounded more exciting than her current responsibility. There was quite the collection of empty boxes on her checklist.

Saying no was just not an option for Sarah. Her interpretation of denying assistance was equal to rejecting the person, and she refused to leave anyone feeling rejected.

For this reason, she was always late to work, slipping through the back door into events or fully armed with excuses for her tardiness to meetings. It was not because she was disrespectful or lazy, but because she was always finding herself lacking enough time to fulfill her commitments. Flying by the seat of her pants became the norm. She was a great person, yet she found herself incompetent in the role her employer had placed her in.

Not until after they fired her did the office realize they'd lost something special when Sarah left.

After they engaged me as a consultant, the manager told me, "I had to fire her. She's a wonderful person, and everyone likes her, but she just didn't get the work done." She disclosed instances of others having to cover for her. Those who were doing her job began to resent it, and ultimately their respect for the manager began to wane. The manager knew her leadership was being questioned by her team and felt she had to make the difficult decision to let Sarah go. I could see her second-guessing her decision as she said, "In short, we couldn't depend on her to carry the load." Although the decision had already been executed, I was there to assess the team. They knew something was missing.

Once I had a good grasp of how their office worked, I realized two things. First, they needed Sarah. She was like a morale officer in the military. She kept the rest of the team smiling and contributed to the bright atmosphere desperately needed at the company. Second, they needed to put her in the right job. Remember the statement in one of my earlier chapters—it's not the right person for the job, it's the right job for the person. Her contribution was not measured in the sales and the bottom line; it was measured in the morale of those who were creating the sales and the bottom line. Her value was essential to the overall team, but it had to be measured differently than that of the other team members. Squeezing her into a role that did not suit her created unrealistic expectations that Sarah was not wired to meet. Once we clarified her strengths, we created a job description that would reinforce her natural gifts.

"We'll call her 'First impressions,'" the team leader said. "She will sit at the receptionist desk and welcome every person who enters with her big, contagious smile and genuine heart-felt charm." She was perfect to disarm the stressful nerves of any guest. New faces did not create discomfort for Sarah; new faces just meant new friends. New friends led to new conversations and new discoveries. This was the excitement she was wired for.

Now at her desk, Sarah only has a phone and a laptop because if she had anything else, it would just become a collection of disorganization, complete with missing items buried under piles of random papers. Her job is being the first impression; thus, it is important for visitors to see a clutter-free desk. Clutter creates chaos. Chaos elevates blood pressure and increases stress. It's one thing to have mountains of paperwork behind the closed door of an office, but this sort of image in the open space of a lobby or front office is not a great way to make a first impression. It subconsciously sends the message that the entire company is in chaos and untrustworthy.

Initially her team supplied her with Post-it Notes, but before the end of her first day welcoming guests, her laptop was buried in small, yellow and green Post-its. When things were slow, she doodled or drew pictures on them—and stuck them all around her desk. It was quite the artistic collage, yet not the purpose for them at the office. Soon a spiral notebook replaced them. She was free to doodle to her heart's content.

"She needs something to do in the down minutes," a team member said. "How about giving her greeting cards?"

"Good idea," everyone said.

Sarah beamed when they gave her a box of assorted cards, and she even adhered to her specific instructions: "Just leave the box inside your desk and only write one card at a time."

She wrote and mailed thank-you cards to clients, personalizing them and expressing appreciation for their business. She wrote thinking-of-you cards or notes to fellow employees that said, "You're doing an amazing job," and slipped them under their doors or onto their desks. When anyone was sick or lost a loved one, Sarah sent get-well or sympathy cards.

Sarah did an excellent job as she used her major gift of relating to others. Everyone who walked through that door—from the UPS delivery person to the water-bottle filler to the copier repairer and, of course, the clients—first got to see Sarah. Even when they didn't say it, they felt they were on top of the world after interacting with her.

"No matter how bad I feel when I enter the business," a messenger said, "after even the briefest interaction with Sarah, I leave feeling better."

Sarah is what we call a High I. Call her a cheerleader or leader of the joy squad, because that's who she is. About 11 percent of the population fit into that category. They may not be known for their vast accomplishments, but they are most definitely known. They make the atmosphere brighter and easier for everyone. They are natural icebreakers. They rarely enter a room without being noticed. In the spotlight is where they shine. If you make eye contact with a High I, you might as well prepare yourself for a conversation, welcomed or not. They love to talk and will do so until they find a common thread that will forever keep you linked.

Lacking at least one I in your business, you could be losing clients without knowing why. I'll tell you a story a friend of mine shared with me to illustrate this point.

"My daughter has a poodle who needed grooming," said my friend. "Less than a mile down the road is a pet groomer with good hours and reasonable prices. My daughter said she likes his work, but the man who runs the place is never happy. Since he never smiles, it's not fun to go there. So my daughter went to a place six miles away that does a less skillful job but is friendly and warm."

The first groomer is losing customers because they lack someone to present a sincerely friendly and kind first impression. It would not be fair to expect the owner—who may be an excellent groomer and businessman—to become someone he's not. He is not wired to present that first, friendly face. Instead of making him fit into a box not his size, he should look to bring on board an I—someone who is energized from personal interaction. Most likely, the owner is a C type, and we'll get into this deeper in a few chapters. He's absorbed with his art of grooming. He can't be interrupted because the finished image of the animal lies within his shears-holding hands. He cannot afford to make a mistake, so looking up to greet others with a smile is not a priority.

Yet he needs someone like a Sarah to warmly welcome the customers and their furry family members. Someone who will make them feel at ease as they release their animal into the care of another. For some, the High I seems very flighty and nonproductive; however, they have their strengths. One of them is the ability to converse with just about anyone in an inclusive, not intrusive, way. They love to include everyone.

Like the D style, the I type is extroverted and doesn't wait for others to interact. They take the initiative. "She never met a stranger" is one way to describe an I. They can walk through a business office or a hospital and make everyone feel comfortable and valued.

Previously, I listed three descriptive words for Sarah types: Inspiring, Innovative, and Impulsive. I could add words like Influencer, Independent, and Igniter.

Every group, every gathering needs at least one I. They're great at hosting dinners, banquets, or parties. They have that natural ability to make others feel good about themselves. Their jaws get a workout every day because they're talking so much and having a great time.

I'm reminded of a conversation I had with another friend. I was in his office when Dave, his partner, returned from lunch. He breezed through, waved at us, and smiled.

My friend said, "I can always tell when Dave has been to lunch with his best friend. He comes back lighthearted and buoyant. It's like he's been somehow lifted out of the mundane and can see the positives in the world again."

The I temperament is great in front of people. They're outstanding onstage and tend to be good at sales because they make people feel important. Their enthusiasm is contagious, and they have a great sense of humor. Often in crisis situations, the I finds something humorous in it and makes everybody laugh, easing tensions and creating an atmosphere where good decisions can be made.

Although most of the time the I types aren't good at following through, they're amazing igniters and awesome when it comes to getting things off to a great start. An I is wired for ideas and creativity.

Limitations of an I

One limitation of an I is that they often appear a bit scatterbrained. They rush home from work because they have an event to attend. They would have been home sooner, but they got caught up in a great conversation as they were leaving the office. Now they are rushing around, searching for that one, outfit-completing clothing item that will make them the standout at the event. The item is buried under a pile of clothes that didn't quite make the fashionable-enough list. No big deal, "Better late than ugly," so they continue the search. Suddenly a text comes in from their boss saying they failed to send an email to meet a deadline. Frantically searching for their laptop, they see their car keys on the pile of clothing. As they reach down to pick up their keys, they are unbelievably reunited with the standout piece of clothing. Overwhelmed by their sudden good luck, they let out a sigh of relief, then remember that in their haste, they left their laptop in the car.

The I types often fail to create margin in their lives, so they are most often feasting on adrenaline from always being in a hurry. This is not an overall healthy pattern, and it can become detrimental to the biological health of the body.

Another limitation is that they are impulsive. Whether buying something in the excitement of the moment and regretting it later, or selling something that may have been valuable to someone else, impulsive decisions usually come at a high price

My kids are now adults, but when younger, it was a common adventure to search for lost shoes all over the house. Someone would inevitably move the shoes out of their way, and then another would slide them further away out of their path, so off we would go on a personal tour of the Chambers crib. It was amazing where some shoes ended up. Under couches, in the cleaning closet, even at the bottom of the toy box—the recovery of that matching flip-flop always brought such a sense of relief and celebration.

In fact, I learned a whole lot about my children when I recruited them to the search and rescue team. "Help me look for Isaac's football shoes, please." Well, they did what I asked for; they literally looked up from their video game or whatever held their attention at that moment, turned their head around as if to peruse the room, and then replied, "Yeah, I just looked for them. I don't see them anywhere." It was amazing how their X-ray vision could operate without even moving their legs. Now, if it happened to be one of their precious items that went missing, they suddenly found a new passion to actually *search* and not just *look*.

Over time, it became evident that we should identify a specific place for shoes. That may sound like a commonsense idea, yet it is very surprising how many moments in our lifetimes are wasted on investigating a case of the missing shoes. Currently, a basket rests at my front door for my now adult children and grandchildren to place their shoes in when they enter. I'm certain it has prevented family feuds when it comes time for them to head home.

Messy rooms, cluttered cars, endless searches for misplaced homework—some of these were only normal teenager character-istics—but four out of my tribe of five had some degree of I behavioral style. Family dinners were full of conversation. You had to learn to listen carefully or you would miss the quick wit and feel left out of the roaring laughter. Plenty of interruptions occurred that inevitably left someone feeling ignored or overlooked. I should thank my kids for my self-educated counseling degree.

Now that four of the five are married and most with their own children, their organizational skills have grown. I love walking into my oldest son's house and seeing an entire space dedicated to housing all their shoes. For some of my kids, the choice to change their behavior came as the result of frustration over the conse-quence of their limitations. For others, their change came at the encouragement of their spouse. Most of my kids, like me, married someone who is wired differently than they are, which truly has proven to be a blessing.

Most of the time the I style is more interested in people than in processes. So when they enter a room, they see who's there. They drop their handbags, their keys, and even their cell phones wherever so they can rush to say hello to all who are in the room. As soon as a new person arrives, the I will immediately leave the conversation and rush over to greet the new attender. Unfortunately, depending on the point of exit, the current communicator might feel their conversation was not exciting enough to maintain the I's attention. Over time, this can leave the one left in the dust to contend with a feeling of insignificance.

The I doesn't intend to make anyone feel rejected. Rejection is their own personal greatest fear. Their expeditious jaunt is merely an attempt to make others feel welcome and included. This is why the I types make the greatest salespeople.

After hours of conversation, the memory of where they unloaded their personal items seems to have been wiped. It helps to do the "where was the last place you remember having your cell phone" exercise: Close your eyes and try to visualize the last time you held it in your hands. Give it a few moments and suddenly the memory card is restored.

The I types are also guilty of procrastination. They are motivated by what will get them noticed. If it's boring or mundane, they just put it off. Remember, they prioritize socialization. They draw energy from people. They do not like to be alone. If you need them to do a task, give them a team or at least someone to do that task with. The more the merrier. Turning a task into a party is a sure way to get them motivated to complete the task.

I, too, am an I, even if it's not my dominant style. I am guilty of rushing into the grocery store parking lot while talking on my cell phone. All is well until I step out of the store, cart full of groceries, and suddenly discover a sea of parked vehicles staring back at me. Trying to remember where I parked sometimes requires an investigative walk throughout the parking lot. Then there is that "light bulb above the head" moment when I recall the lock feature on my key fob always honks my horn when clicked. So now, in a sea of parked cars, I just honk to myself when necessary. Even the car manufacturers recognize there are some of us who really need assistance in life.

Recognizing my own I behavior, I have discovered all kinds of "save the brain" shortcuts. In many seasons, we traveled so often that I would confuse my hotel room numbers with those of previous trips. It's terrible to find yourself staring into the face of someone occupying your hotel room, only to discover you were trying to force your new key into the door with the room number you stayed in the week before. The occupant wasn't in the wrong room, I was. So I now take a quick picture of my hotel room number as I leave the room. I do the same when parking in a parking garage; I just snap a quick picture of the parking space number, and then I'm free to explore the world with confidence that I will find my way back.

If You Are an I

You make friends quickly and easily. You're a real people person. For you, it's impossible to walk down the hall without saying hello to everyone. As a natural and ingrained habit, it's something you do every morning. If the other person is obviously busy, you smile and wave. Remember this: if they do not look up from their computer to return the smile, don't take it as rejection. Just come back later after they've finished the task at hand.

Try to be patient. If you have a question—one that seems vitally important—avoid interrupting the entire group by shouting your inquiry from across the room. First, move in closer. And by all means, give someone a chance to answer your question before you ask another. What is urgent to you is not always a matter of life or death to others. My mother used to tell me, "Jill, the whole world does not revolve around you." It was a shocking realization, but I did finally accept it.

"I'm sorry, I just blurt things out," my friend told me. "I'm just afraid I'll forget what I'm going to say so I just say it." Holding your tongue is an exercise in wisdom. Be courteous, look around the room, assess the situation before you just blow in, blow up, and blow out. If people are conversing, let them come to a complete stop before you roll into their intersection and cause a communication collision.

You're the energy machine. When they're around you, others become alive and draw vitality from you. Just remember to take time to recharge your energy. Don't view alone time as lonely time. Even though you are an extrovert and love people, taking time for self-care and inner evaluation is important. Keeping yourself busy might just be an excuse for putting off things that really need your attention. One of my mentors taught me to never confuse activity with accomplishment. Filling every moment on your calendar does not make you look important. It actually contributes to your constant rushing around and the never-ending feeling of having to catch up. Down time isn't wasted time. Think about it: you can't inhale and talk at the same time. That's how God created us. Take time to fill your lungs as well as your heart and your mind.

As a natural life enthusiast, you get visits and calls from people who tell you, "I was having a down day and needed someone to give me a lift. Thank you." You enjoy and accept the compliment, but you probably also wonder what you did to make them feel that way. You are truly gifted at brightening the atmosphere around you wherever you go. You influence others because of your bubbly, upbeat attitude. You've probably been asked, "Are you ever down?"

With a silver-lining lens on the world, you find it very difficult when storms hit. You will feel down some days, although not many, but they will be there. If you find yourself in the middle of a down day, just remember it's not getting knocked down that's tragic, it's staying down. Just dust yourself off and get back up. You don't win or lose in this life; you win or learn.

It's important for you to be liked by everyone. Because your greatest fear is being rejected, you will go out of your way to get others to like you. Just be cautious of compromising your character to get that approval. Many Is struggle with approval addiction. This can become very unhealthy if you constantly find yourself trying to please people with your acts of service. Over time, a string will become attached at the end of your gesture and you might find yourself constantly feeling like they owe you. If your generosity comes with a silent, *Now it's your turn to do something for me,* you are not really being generous. Don't allow your act of kindness to be an undercover masquerade for a desperate need for attention.

Learning to love yourself for who you are regardless of who notices you is essential to you living your best life. If you live for the applause of others, you will die from the lack of it. No amount of applause will give you a genuine sense of purpose. You are amazing. You don't have to be the center of attention all of the time. If you are an I, share the spotlight. Give someone else the floor. Use your words to brag on others instead of talking about yourself. You don't need to drop names or talk about who you know to get people to like you. You are enough all by yourself.

Interacting with an I Style

▸ Encourage them to express their thoughts and emotions.

▸ Remind yourself that they need to be the center of attention—that's how they are wired.

▸ Keep the conversation light.

▸ If a situation becomes tense, the I in the crowd is most often quick to make a joke and to get people laughing.

▸ They're warm and informal. Respond in the same way.

▸ If you want something specific from them, write it down or text them. They tend to be forgetful because they're caught up in the moment. They don't easily follow through, so you most likely will have to follow up with them to be sure they are getting the job done.

▸ From a negative perspective, they're restless and can be obnoxious without meaning to be.

▸ Despite their upbeat persona, they often anger easily.

▸ They have a "feeling" style and often come across as naive.

▸ They don't mask their emotions because they don't know how. Their bodies, voices, and gestures tell others exactly how they feel.

▸ Tread carefully with criticism; they're afraid of not being liked. Your disapproval becomes personal and says to them, "I don't like you."

- Clarity is a big issue; they're afraid of being misunderstood.

- They are wired with a spontaneous sense of humor and easily bring levity in the conversation. The challenge is that it may not be appropriate in the moment. Otherwise, they can come across as disrespectful.

- They typically want to help people. They often overcommit and answer, "Yes, yes, yes, yes, yes." Afterward, they moan, "Oh no! I've got two appointments at the same time. Which one do I go to?"

- Because of the way they're wired, many of them tend to be jealous of others quicker than any other temperament.

- The High I tends to be egocentric. They exaggerate and talk a lot.

- They love to share. The worst thing you can do is shut them down. Allow them to speak but *gently* remind them they're not the only one in the room and others need to talk. "That's a great story," you say when they pause. "And how about Linda? You want to share something with us?"

- With an I, you need to break tasks down into next steps. That is, you explain how to start and then say, "Next, you . . ." and continue to add *next* until you've laid out the steps. Don't just *say* the words. Write them out, or have the I write them out. Otherwise, they get distracted or procrastinate.

- Learn to accept the fact that an I doesn't always finish what they start. When giving them assignments, ask, "Is this the best way for you to start?" Get them going with their creativity, and arrange for someone else to *polish* (a polite way to say *finish*) the job.

CHAPTER SEVEN

Steady S

On treadmills at the gym, two people are walking side by side. Five minutes ago, they were strangers. Then the man on the right says, "I've seen you in here before. How often do you come?"

The woman to his left replies, "A couple times a week."

From then on, and for as long as both are on their respective treadmills, the conversation never lags, especially from the I—the man on the right. He tells his life story or some long, personal experience and probably runs out of breath. The walker on the left gets a good workout because she's listening. She may share a few stories but doesn't lead or dominate the conversation.

Both are people oriented, but the I is extroverted. The woman on the left is the quieter one; you call her an introvert. Because the woman on the left mostly listens, she's probably a High S and used to having people say, "You're a good listener."

And why not? She's wired that way. Not only is she a fine listener, but you can also call her steady, stable, and secure.

If you're familiar with the expression, "Still waters run deep," that's an apt description of an S. Because of their basic nature, S types are easy to talk to, often because they're the opposite of the I. They prefer to use their ears to listen rather than use their mouths to talk. That's important for you to know when you're working with a team; you don't want it filled solely with D and I behaviors. Because of their outgoing and extrovert behaviors, it might seem easy to heavily recruit these styles. The truth is, the D types need someone to carry out their directives and the I types need someone who will listen to them—and for many other reasons as well.

The S types must have invented the saying, "Keep calm and carry on." By behaving this way, they provide a calming effect in a group because of their stability. Further, they tend to be relaxed and down-to-earth; you don't hear them chattering. They're balanced people who make you feel secure. The High S is eager to help, and once that person offers to assist, you can rely on a follow-through.

The S behavioral style covers about 69 percent of the population. That is by far the largest of the four DISC personalities. If you are not an S yourself, you most likely have one in your family. You probably work with an S. They provide the other three personalities—the D, I, and C—with support.

Their strength is that they are definitely likable and super diplomatic; they care about people, and they want everyone to have a good experience. Along with that, they're wired for efficiency. They don't usually need to be the leader; consequently, they make excellent supporters. They're quiet but witty, which makes me think of my dad, who's a High S. He's hilarious when he chooses to express humor. When I was growing up, I remember wanting to be in the room where adults were conversing. There would always be a moment when, after sitting in silence, my dad would say something brilliant or at least brilliantly funny. I would sit and wait patiently just to hear his quick-witted response. In fact, he would say it so fast most wouldn't even catch it. I grew up with one sister, so Dad had three women in the house—it's definitely a good thing he was patient and laid-back.

Human resources departments consider the S style as good employees because they're dependable and able to do routine work carefully and patiently. They also have a strong bent for practicality. Especially prized is their ability to meet deadlines, which keeps the process flowing.

Someone illustrated the S type by using the analogy of a canoe. The D and I styles remain standing the entire time, but an S gets into the canoe, sits down, and reaches for an oar. That steadies the canoe and puts it in motion toward its destination.

Unlike the I, they don't do well with superficial relationships. Instead, they're the people who have fewer but deeper relationships. They get along with many people but are very self-protective. They take great care to only be transparent with those they deeply trust.

While the D and I are usually clear about what they believe and stand for, the S types rarely offer their opinions or share their deepest beliefs. They recognize that the extroverts love to debate and talk out their thoughts. Conflict threatens the peace, so they often remain silent. Don't confuse their silence with lack of passion. Their internal dialogue is as witty and brilliant as their outward humor. Because they reserve their energy for thinking instead of talking, sarcasm naturally takes on its greatest form as time passes by. It's very common for the S to stand for *shredding*. If unchecked, they can verbally dice their opponent into minced meat.

Because my dominant behavioral style is S, early in my marriage I found myself constantly restraining my mouth to keep the peace. But in a battle of wits with me, Danny would often share that he felt unarmed. Over time I realized that my words truly carried weight with my husband, my children, and others. In fact, if you could just be in my head and see the brilliant arsenal of comebacks I've collected over the years, you would most likely run away. Let me assure you, they are my private collection and I intentionally keep them under mental lock and key. Every now and then one slips out, forcing me to go on a repentance campaign. Because people are valuable to me and because my core value is honor, it's unacceptable for me to use my wit and my words to cut down or devalue others.

The S style is wired for security and safety. This enables them to keep distance between themselves and the assertive, outgoing types. You can count on the S style. When you hand them an assignment, you sense they'll do a good job. They tend to resist change, however, and if the assignment is highly innovative or outside the usual way things are done, you're likely to get resistance. They do not like taking risks and will choose the long way if it happens to be the safest. While Ds and Is are quick to jump on a bandwagon, S will wait to see how it works for others first.

For example, a generation ago there were the people who balked at learning to use something new called the computer. "What's wrong with the way things are?" they asked. A friend once told me that a client of his in 1998 balked at the idea of building a website for their ministry. "The internet is just a fad," said the client. The future can be very unsettling for an S.

An S is liked for being loyal and full of common sense. At work they tend to identify strongly with team goals and work to build relationships. You probably know them as the dependable, capable people who don't care to forge ahead in their careers. Although they don't say the words aloud (and may not even be aware of it themselves), they desire the safety of what they've been doing rather than the uncertainty of a new position or job move. "Why should I move on?" says the I. "I like the work I'm doing."

Although they are self-sacrificing, they can also tend to slip into a martyr syndrome. They are not easily upset, and they are good under pressure. Word to the wise: do not push or try to pressure an S into action. Unlike the D, they do not thrive with a challenge. An I will succumb to peer pressure just to fit in. But the S will not be moved. The harder you push, the more they push back. Feeling forced to make a move or decision just breeds suspicion: "Why are you pushing me?" They are unwilling to sacrifice their own safety and security or that of those they love.

Once on the TV show *Dr. Phil*, a woman complained about her husband never opening up. "He works hard and provides well for the family." Then she said, "When just the two of us are on vacation, in any one day, he doesn't say more than a hundred words." She compared him to the tall, silent hero in western movies.

I don't remember everything from that show, but when the husband finally opened up, he explained that his family moved a lot because his father couldn't hold a job for more than a few months. "I attended fourteen different schools. Sixth grade was the only time I stayed in the same class for a full year." He pointed out that if he remained quiet (or as he said, "invisible") no one laughed at him. Dr. Phil pointed out that the husband had experienced a traumatic childhood, so he learned "to play it safe" in releasing personal information. By remaining silent, he learned to fit in with the flow of school events.

Another significant quality of S behavior is that closure is necessary when they take on a task. Their mentality says, "Whatever I start, I have to finish." That sometimes puts a heavy burden on them. They refuse to be identified as a quitter. This is very admirable in many ways; just be aware it is also a reason to put off starting something. Without the promise of a finish line, they will not begin the race. Sometimes painfully slow to get moving is the result of the mental tug-of-war between the risk of change and the comfort of routine.

If you are wired as an S, you generally make an excellent parent. You enjoy doing school projects with your kids. You'll stay up all night to see the completion of the creation, even if you end up finishing it while your child passes out at the table. It's not uncommon for an S parent to inquire of the child, "How did *we* do on our project?" and go out for ice cream to celebrate the great accomplishment no matter the grade given.

You're not in a hurry. Again, I think of my father. On the occasions when I felt rushed and began to panic, he asked, "Why are you in such a hurry? It took your whole life to get here." That caused me to laugh; I relaxed and slowed down.

Characteristically, S types are limited by their insecurity. I'm a High S and still experience that feeling often. I've had to overcome that insecurity which leads to guilt and self-condemnation. Knowing my limitations helped enable me to accept myself that way and grasp how it affects my behavior. DISC mentoring by

Dr. Sandy Kulkin and leadership mentoring with John Maxwell enabled me to face my insecurities and uncertainties.

My husband also constantly stretched me beyond my insecurities.

Danny was singing at a huge youth conference at Lakewood Church when the late John Osteen was still at the helm. It was our first large event after we were married. I was so nervous watching him onstage. *How does he do it?* I asked myself. *He's so comfortable in front of people on the stage.* I began to wonder what my contribution would be in our ministry career together. *I could never do that; stand on a stage in front of people.* I was sitting on the second row right behind Joel Osteen's mother, Dodie. The mind monsters of inadequacy were raging in my head. All of a sudden, as if she could hear my thoughts, Miss Dodie turned around, grabbed my hands, looked me in the eye, and said, "Honey, is that your husband up there on that stage?" I answered a shy, Southern, "Yes, ma'am." She then proceeded to say with confidence and assurance, "You belong up there right by his side." Her words still resonate with me to this day.

The first time Danny asked me to sing with him onstage in front of people, I almost threw up. We actually found old VHS tapes of some of our conferences from back in the early 1990s where I first performed with him. I was like a wallflower at the high school prom. I stood as far back on the stage as I could—I took "background singer" literally. Thank God for people who not only saw potential in me but who also called it out. This was over thirty years ago. I still have to overcome the mind monsters of insecurity, but it doesn't take me as long to rise up as it used to. The awareness of my limitation has given me the courage to choose to be brave.

Among an S's strengths are the ability to take the good with the bad. "She wears well," someone said of an S who worked with us, and that fit nicely. "She rarely caused any problems and got along with every member of the team," was mentioned in her exit interview.

An S is wired to be calm under pressure. In a crisis, they remain unruffled as they find a simple, straightforward solution to the problem. They value peace, and therefore bring peace into chaos. It's not uncommon for an "SIC" combination behavioral style to be identified as a D in crisis. They are quick to jump in, leading a calculated and decisive plan for resolution. Because they are motivated by peace, they do whatever it takes to create a peaceful end. This combination makes a great team member. They are happy to follow and support the leader, yet, in necessary times, they step up to lead.

A limitation they face is the avoidance of conflict. They don't like arguments and will do whatever they can to defuse controversy and clashes with others. Sometimes they come across as stubborn and self-righteous because they do tend to judge others by their often-inflexible standards. "Silently stubborn" is a great description; not tempted to engage in debate yet unmovable in their belief. This is a great asset when holding fast to one's conviction. Yet when deciding on a lesser issue, it may seem like *Mission: Impossible* to get them to change their mind. As an S myself, let me give you hope. Proving to them the security and safety of a matter even amid certain risks is not completely impossible. It just takes patience. Replace your pushiness with patience, and you will more likely stand a chance.

When antagonized, they passive-aggressively withdraw and seek to blend in. Over time they may forgive, but they rarely forget. They're the people who say, "I haven't forgotten how you . . ." and name some personal infringement that might have happened two years earlier. Their loyalty to those they deeply love may cause them to harbor secondhand offense. This second-hand offense is often more challenging to get over than their own personal offense.

Over the years, I have had to release forgiveness on many occasions. I'm sure you have too. People can just be mean. As I realized that my forgiveness did not excuse the ill behavior of others but released me from the negative energy of carrying the offense, it became easier to forgive.

In his book, *Deadly Emotions,* my friend, Dr. Don Colbert, scientifically shows that harboring a grudge and holding on to past offenses decreases the immune system, opening the body to all kinds of disease.

If you find your memory card full of offense, let me encourage you to have the courage to forgive. I've been in numerous life-coaching sessions where my clients have allowed the words of someone who was six feet under to remain in control of their thoughts. The person is no longer living yet still dictating their lives.

At times the S seems to withdraw, which usually means they don't want to take sides in any disagreement. Neutrality is their stance, sometimes interpreted as indifference. They're caring people and want everyone to have a good experience. Because of that caring ability, they can usually take the good with the bad and aren't easily upset. But you have to watch them because they're not goal oriented.

"What do you think about that?" they may ask, and it's not an idle question. The S wants to know what *you* think. They probably haven't yet formed an opinion themselves and await your reply to help them decide.

My family laughs at me because, as an S, when we eat in a restaurant, Danny or one of the others will unconsciously ask, "What are you ordering?" I mumble or continue to skim the menu, especially in a restaurant that's new to me. I gravitate toward security, and it shows in what I finally order—something simple that the chef likely won't mess up. Conversely, Danny inevitably asks the server, "What is the best thing on the menu?" In other words, he wants to know the most popular thing to order. Upon their answer, he then asks, "What is your favorite thing on the menu?" Reading expressions doesn't require a degree when you choose to listen with both your ears and your eyes. If they are uninspired by the most popular menu item, you will see it expressed on their face. Their tone of voice is a dead giveaway that just because it's popular doesn't mean it's tasty.

It's amazing to see the sparkle in their eyes when they share their favorite selection.

Taking his cues from the server's experience has landed my husband an undefeated record in the winning dinner choices category. I will admit, my risk-taking husband has tried some very interesting meals across the globe, but he still remains the meal champion. Even in foreign countries like Cambodia where he actually ate a tarantula, he wins as the daring rock star without fear. Me, I just took a picture holding one. Absolutely no regret here!

The S likes routine, repeated work patterns rather than having to learn something new. For example, everyone in the office gets notified of an update on their computer operating system or an upgrade on their cell phone. A typical response for an S, and this is true with me, is to put off installing the update as long as they can. I'm one of the last ones to update. I think, *What if it completely messes up my phone?* Honestly, I usually just get the hang of the changes when it's time to update again.

The S definitely wants to be identified within the group and not to be overlooked, but they typically don't want to lead. They don't mind more work, but they don't want to be overloaded because they don't want to fail. By contrast, they're willing to help you with *your* responsibility. It's as if they say, "I'll be your right-hand person, but please don't make me responsible for the project."

Confronting an S can be hazardous because of their avoidance of conflict. Their greatest fear is loss of security. Confrontation is often seen as a threat, so it is vital that you replace the word *confront* with *clarify*. Getting clarity is less intimidating and simply sounds more peaceful.

In my workplace, I've learned not to confront an S with, "What did you do? Why did you do that?" Rather, I say, "Help me understand what happened." I use the words *help me understand* more than once. "Help me understand what you were thinking." "Help me understand why you took that action." Nothing accusatory, and I keep it relational. This appeals to the helpful nature of the S. It's setting them up to assist in clarity rather than armor up to protect their territory. My purpose is to create a favorable and agreeable environment so I can better understand their behavior. And in doing so, I genuinely express interest, reminding myself that person needs to feel appreciated and included.

Because the S doesn't easily offer opinions, they need to be encouraged to share. Because they are thinkers and introverted by nature, they usually have good ideas. Unfortunately, they will take them to their grave unless someone sees their value and takes time to go dig them out. *They don't really care what I think.* This is an all-too-common thought of someone who struggles believing in their own ideas. "I don't want to be a bother or inconvenience anyone" can seem on the surface to be very passive-aggressive, yet it could also just be that they don't want to appear on the "needy" list.

I've had to learn to be patient and wait for the person to feel comfortable enough to speak. Even though I don't say this in words, as an S myself, I want them to hear, "I'm not withholding information or trying to hide something from you." The reality is that I withhold information until I figure out what I want to say.

I remind myself not to rush the person. Impatience may cause them to think, *She really doesn't care or she'd give me time to reflect before I answer.* Patience is a gift because it allows time to draw out their ideas and their position, and it allows them to tell me what they wanted to accomplish in the situation.

Early in my career in working the DISC profile, I discovered the importance of intentionally creating a feeling or atmosphere of security. Even in an insecure environment, it's vital to seek at least something that can bring reassurance. As an employer, I recognized the power of clear expectations and understandable direction. These bring confidence to the S to move forward. They live in a yellow-light mindset: "Proceed with Caution." It's not a bad thing, it's a real thing. Sometimes their caution can even prevent a collision in your family, church, or company.

I remember being first in the left-turn lane at a stoplight years ago. The light transitioned from red to green, and for some reason, I hesitated. The blaring honk from the driver behind me confirmed their lack of patience. Startled at their boldness and apologetic for their inconvenience, I slowly moved my foot from the brake to the gas. Just as I began to enter the intersection, a silver SUV rushed through the intersection. I noticed the driver was on his cell phone, completely unaware that his light had turned red. My "Proceed with Caution" was validated by Dad's voice in my head as flashbacks of neighborhood driving lessons flooded my mind. "Jill, you have to drive defensively. If you act as if everyone else is distracted and not paying attention, you will most likely drive safer and arrive in one piece." His wisdom set me up to be more aware of the drivers around me. And on this particular day, it worked. My hesitation became the very thing that protected me from getting hit.

Not to offer clear instructions reminds me of ushers at church. They are there to guide people where to sit, especially in a crowded sanctuary. The usher who understands and recognizes how people are wired differently will execute their responsibilities much more successfully. A D walks in and goes straight to the seat they feel is the best. A simple nod from the usher means they have been given permission to pick their seat. The I scans the room for friends and goes and sits with them. Their experience is determined by *who* they are with. The C has *their* seat that they are most likely already sitting in because they were early enough to ensure they would get to sit in their spot. But the S needs to be guided to a seat. They don't want to sit in someone else's seat or inconvenience anyone.

But what if the usher said, "Oh, just sit anyplace you can find a spot"? The S won't ask the usher, "Where do you want me to sit?" even though that's what they really prefer. They feel they shouldn't have to ask, and they don't want to frustrate or inconvenience the usher. Without guidance, they feel uncertain. Their response to the usher is not to return to that church.

If You Are an S

You are

- known as a team player,
- friendly with colleagues and supervisors,
- diplomatic because you don't want to hurt feelings,
- conservative and comfortable in the way things have always been done,
- sometimes seen as judgmental or self-righteous,
- reluctant to take leadership roles,
- good under pressure but resent being pushed,
- may be called poker faced because others can't see how you feel.

Interacting with an S Style

- Recognize their loyalty, commitment, and service.

▶ Remind yourself not to be put off or take it as a negative if the S shows no emotion when talking or listening.

▶ Show openness to avoid being perceived as competitive or aggressive.

▶ Clearly explain exactly what you expect of them.

▶ While appreciating their easygoingness, be aware that when pushed, they can become passive-aggressive, saying, "Yes, but . . ."

▶ Remind yourself that S is wired for secure situations and needs sincere appreciation.

▶ An S needs and welcomes follow-up. Check to see how they're doing, and encourage them to keep going.

The higher the S score on the assessment, the higher the intensity of these characteristics. You might find yourself identifying with some of these descriptions more than others, but it's rare that these identifiers will become your entire biography. More likely, you will connect to portions of the descriptions. Your honesty with yourself is vital to your ability to choose to change your behavior. Because 69 percent of people identify with some part of the S style, the likelihood of you, the reader, connecting to this chapter is very high. I pray you do not disconnect from any further chapters because you feel they won't relate to you. Read on, to continue learning more about yourself and others.

CHAPTER
EIGHT

Correct C

"Those figures are incorrect," Katherine Goble pointed out after studying a large chalkboard of calculations at NASA headquarters. That scene sets the tone for the film, *Hidden Figures*.

The movie—based on a true story—powerfully shows several C types in action. They're all Black women working in segregated situations. Their ability to compute figures quickly and accurately enables them to correct calculations by top mathematicians during the space race in the late 1950s. Because of her acuity with numbers, Goble moves forward, against racist and anti-female prejudice. Her calculations were used for John Glenn to become the first American to orbit the earth in 1962. Katherine Goble calculated the trajectories for the Apollo 11 and space shuttle missions. In 2015, she was awarded the Presidential Medal of Freedom. The following year, NASA's Langley Research Center in Hampton, Virginia, named its new building after her.

Goble is a marvelous example of the High C. People like her are wired to offer precise details about whatever they work on. Along with that, they like to follow rules, both in their personal and private lives. They're highly analytic, stable, and dependable. Another way to say it is that they're excellent problem solvers. When they focus on a task, they grasp details that others tend to miss.

Their strong drive to be right pushes them to spend time researching and rethinking every aspect of a situation. That ability leads them to high standards for efficiency.

Normally, the C is adaptable and peaceful. They have the amazing ability to assess new situations objectively. They are wired to be correct, calculated, cautious, and conscientious. Even though it doesn't fit the alliteration, I'd have to add *reserved* and *task oriented*. They represent about 17 percent of the population.

Because of their abilities, they often come across as too precise, neat, and exacting for most people. "You're such a perfectionist," others say to C—meant as a put-down but received as a compliment.

And like the S type, they resist change. "We never did it that way before," is one of their protests. "This is the way we've always done it, and it works, so why do it differently?" While the S will usually give in for the sake of peace, the C will do everything they can to avoid compliance at the cost of correctness.

Criticism is their greatest fear, yet they tend to emit a critical attitude. Often when ideas are shared, their first response may seem like a wet blanket snuffing out the creative fire of ingenuity. The intent is not to deflate the room. They are wired to foresee challenges and potential obstacles. This can be quite the asset in preventing unnecessary spending or even wasted energy on a dead-end street. Understanding the strength of the C is essential to your success in relating to them. Once you understand their deep conviction regarding correctness, you will better understand their contribution. Being right is not always about being the best; it is literally about being correct.

Leading a nonprofit organization for over three decades brought my husband and me quite the awareness for the importance of correctness. Managing the contributions of hardworking people is not something to be taken lightly. Maintaining the financial integrity of any organization takes great intention.

For over twenty-two years, my husband and I led a thriving church. We were given three churches and found ourselves at one time leading a multisite organization with three separate locations. The scrutiny that churches endure is often painful regarding how moneys are spent. This can seem to be a thorn in the flesh, yet it is one of the main reasons many organizations, including churches, fail. "The devil is in the details" is a saying that rings true. One overlooked detail could cost thousands of dollars or even terminate the nonprofit status.

One of our greatest blessings over the years came to us in the form of Pam. We hired Pam to oversee and manage our finances. Pam is a High C. Her passion for correctness and her diligence in keeping exquisite records qualified our organization to become a certified member of the Evangelical Council for Financial Accountability. One of the many requirements for this status is a yearly self-initiated audit. For almost an entire month every year, Pam would shut herself up in her office with a sign on her door "Audit, audit, audit, if you must knock to ask, have chocolate in hand." The detail in which she ran our financial office was stellar. The policies and procedures were clear and the expectations high. Often the burden she carried in protecting the financial integrity of our church translated into a short, abrupt reply. Understanding her responsibility prevented me from taking her response personally and feeling the need to armor up in defense. Recognizing her strengths and honoring her ability to read and understand the fine print infused a deep, mutual appreciation.

Gathering the information or the facts takes precedence for Cs, and they must be convinced of the correctness of their work before they reach a conclusion. They spend endless time getting to the bottom of a problem, rechecking and reexamining the information. They've been accused of suffering from "analysis paralysis" because they can get stuck focusing on the minutiae.

Wise team leaders applaud them for their loyalty and dedication in completing whatever is assigned to them. And they often point out that the result is excellent.

The C-type personality is wired to pick up after their children. They often prefer an orderly environment and end up removing clutter from their line of sight. Attempting to teach their children to appreciate cleanliness, a C may stack their personal items on the staircase, expecting them to pick up the items and put them where they belong. I myself have attempted the stack-the-staircase theory. Unfortunately, I still had to make a point to ask my children to put their things away. They would find a way to step over a mountainous pile of books while walking upstairs and not even looking down.

I have a little bit of C in me. For example, as my friends Ronnie and Jennifer were finishing their meal at our lunch together one day, I automatically began clearing the plates and setting them on the edge of the table for the waitress. My S wanted to help the server—not that she needed my help—and my C was in protection mode. We were deep in a very personal discussion, absorbed with the topic. It would have seemed awkward for the conversation to be interrupted with, "Are you finished?" or "May I take this out of your way?" My automatic internal-wiring mechanism was to protect the privacy of the discussion by sliding our dishes where they could be easily accessible. My personal mission was a success because no one at the table skipped a beat. Everyone kept to the conversation without interruption.

The C's attention to detail pushes them into positions of quality control. They are naturally gifted and successful proofreaders who immediately spot incorrect spelling or grammar. Protecting the brand is a great strength of theirs. They are literal when following instructions and thrive on clear directions.

A generation ago, a TV commercial showed velvet-voiced actor Orson Welles listening to *Symphony No. 5 in C Minor, Op. 67* on a record player. He pointed out that Beethoven took four years to write it. He paused before he pitched Paul Masson wine, with the famous saying, "Some things can't be rushed." The commercial ended with him quoting the company's slogan, "We will sell no wine before its time." That sounds like a description for a High C.

Some things truly can't be rushed; however, overanalyzing may cause a painful delay in production. In some cases deadlines are missed, not because of laziness but because of perfection. I've worked with employees who invested over thirty hours on a video project and then scrapped the entire thing because in their minds it wasn't good enough. The entire team suffered from intense disappointment and a sense of inadequacy. When I finally got my eyes on the project, I was shocked at its brilliance and deeply saddened by its termination. It was not only good enough, it was great.

C types are also very creative. They can be musically gifted and artistic.

Living in Nashville, I am surrounded by artists and musicians. I've been in the studio with supremely gifted and talented people. It is fascinating to spot the different styles of behavior in these scenarios. Years ago, I was singing background vocals on a project for a new artist. Joining me were two vocalists who were complete opposites. The tenor was a great guy, full of life, and lit up the room. He was an I with a blend of C. The soprano was very serious and meticulous. She had her vocal chart in front of her and was rehearsing her parts endlessly. She was a High C. I was singing alto. We did a quick run-through of the song a few times to confirm our notes and secure our blend. Just before we began to record, the producer came in to make a few changes on the vocal parts for the chorus. As we ran through the updated chorus, the soprano kept hitting a wall. She could not seem to adjust to the change. It was painful. Each time we attempted to record the chorus, she would go deeper and deeper into her mind and overanalyze the change. After many failed attempts, she began to self-criticize. Her overthinking paralyzed her from moving forward, and we eventually had to call in another singer.

Being correct is painful when it's hijacked by perfectionism. There is nothing wrong with having high standards. Just be sure those standards are within reach.

In one of my life-coaching sessions, I asked my client to list her values and standards. A few weeks later she handed me a list titled "He Must." It was a list of her expectations for her future spouse. "He must be kindhearted." I agreed. "He must have a job." I thought this was a good one as well. The further down the list I read, the more I realized, *This man doesn't exist. There is no way humanly possible to meet these standards.* The revelation of why she had not been on a date in years suddenly hit me. Desperately trying to empathize with her while finishing the list, I thought about it for a moment, and then I asked her, "Do you meet the standards on this list yourself?" She looked up at me with deep consideration and then said a convicted, "No, ma'am." With a sense of relief, I smiled and said, "Why don't you remake this list."

Cs often set unrealistic goals for themselves and for others. Self-deprecation is expressed through extreme moodiness. What feels like an all-out assault on others may be the result of their own severe frustration with themselves. If you are a C, give yourself a pass. Forgive, and move forward. Don't remain incarcerated by your own mind monsters. Mistakes are not the unforgivable sin. We all make them. It's time to release yourself and others from the prison of perfectionism.

Cs possess a genuine appreciation for beauty. They are captivated by a breathtaking sunset, a perfectly placed rainbow at the end of a storm, or a classically painted mural. They are very philosophical and poetic. Some of the greatest writers and classical composers like Shakespeare and Beethoven would be identified as C styles.

Depression and loneliness trouble many High Cs. *Am I the only one who understands this dilemma?* they sometimes ask themselves. They fear looking foolish. That can make them appear rigid, cold, and seemingly heartless.

They're very much about making the world go around *correctly* and about staying in their lane on the highway. They're very much about paying the toll and about following the rules.

Like the High D, they're task oriented; however, for them, it's all about getting the work done. More than most people, they care about the task and "doing it right."

In a TV interview, the author of a best-selling book on the history of World War II was asked if he liked the response. "Yes," he said, "except I shudder when I think the publisher allowed it to go into print with three typos."

That's how Cs are wired.

Not only are they self-demanding, they're also quick to correct others. For instance, coming out of church one day, a man shivered and I heard him say, "It must be ten degrees below freezing out here." His companion said, "It's 33—still a degree above freezing."

It's not that Cs don't care about people, they do; but their priority is accuracy. That makes me think of this quotation from the French playwright Pierre Corneille: "The manner of giving is worth more than the gift."

"The manner of giving" isn't high on their priority list. Packaging is not their priority. They spend less time on how they say things because they say things less often. Recognizing that your unpackaged response can come across as cruel and sarcastic is key to changing the way others perceive you. The same words you use to put others down can be adjusted and become a source of encouragement to lift others up.

In the previous chapter, I contrasted an I and S on a treadmill at the gym. To that illustration, I could point out that the person on the third treadmill is a C—walking steadily but with earphones on, as if to hold out a sign saying, "Let me alone while I finish my exercise program." Finishing what they start and finishing without interruption is vital to them.

I highly respect the Cs because I believe it's important to say what you truly, honestly believe to be the case. It's unfortunate that Cs often come across as critical. You see, they're realists. The Cs are the ones who actually know the truth. They know what really happened, they know the real statistics. They have done the research, created the graphs, and worked the figures. They know the real projections. Facts outweigh opinion.

Many times I've said, "If you're going to spend a million dollars to work with a company, you need to know everything about the company. If you're going to invest money into a piece of property, you need to know everything about that property. You need to know the risks and any problems you'll encounter. If you want to build something, you need to know how much the soil test will cost. You need to know how much the architectural drawings will be. In other words, hire a High C."

In behavior, Cs show they're not only analytical but also realistic. When you think of a good architect or general contractor, you think of someone who pays extremely close attention to detail.

Cs sometimes get a bad rap because of their critical eye, but they definitely shine in fields such as engineering, car repair, airplane mechanics, or jobs where people's lives are at stake because they will correctly engineer and build. They're amazing when it comes down to making sure everything is perfect. If you hire someone to build your house, seek a High C because that person will notice the smallest details and won't allow any kind of shoddy workmanship.

I know a contractor who lost money on a building project because the people who laid the carpet in the bonus room measured wrong and tried to cover it with a patch. Even though that patch wasn't obvious to most people, it was there, and he insisted they pull up the entire carpet, get new material, and make it exact.

Cs are self-sacrificing. A lot of times they are self-disciplined. They do tend to come across as serious because they're purposeful, they're focused. A lot of geniuses are Cs.

They're artistic, which can come across as weird when they, like other artists or musicians sometimes do, seem like they are just out there floating in the air not getting anything done, but they're actually working inside their head producing art.

They're not going to impulsively get something done. They're going to research thoroughly because they want to make sure it's the right way, the best way, the most effective way, the most cost-effective way. When planning a major project, having a C on your team is vital. Their research alone can save money and time. Details do not bog them down; on the contrary, they fire them up. If you are that person, let me encourage you: This is your area of strength. A lot of people overlook many, many details.

Let's look at it this way. If you put all four behavioral types in a room, the D is going to dream it up, and the I is going to talk it up. The S is going to help you share it with other people, and the C is going to actually make it happen by pointing out things such as the research, the money, and the liabilities.

One of the best things I learned in business was how to get an I to include Cs at the start of an idea. Doing so gave the Cs affirmation and gave the I the ability to complete the task and receive recognition for it.

A friend I'll call Tracy, who's a High C, was amazing at spotting problems, but at work she drove the rest of the team crazy because she came across as highly critical. For instance, we would sit in a room and listen to our visionary CEO share his idea. When asking for response, she'd provide ten reasons it wouldn't work.

After the third time that happened, I called her into my office. After reminding her that I valued her insight and liked her work, I added, "You make me see and think of things I wouldn't have imagined." I gave her two examples.

"I asked you to come here because you're right on—absolutely correct in your conclusions. You quickly grasp the problems and help us see things more clearly. When you speak, there's no doubt that you've correctly assessed the situation."

By then she was relaxed and nodding.

"Everything you say is always, always correct, but not everyone on the team can look at the issues objectively the way you do."

"I've sure noticed that—"

"It's easy enough to remedy. With your insightful comprehension of the situation, there's one thing I need you to do."

I paused, and she nodded.

"Before you tell us why it *won't* work, give us five reasons why it *will*. And with your unique ability, you can easily do that—" I held up my hand before she objected. "Once you've done that, then you can tell us why it won't work. That way everyone can perceive your objectivity and realize you are not just being negative."

She nodded slowly.

"You have an amazing ability to observe and correctly understand things that the rest of us are blind to. I hope you know how much I appreciate that in you."

Tracy assured me she did and added how much she enjoyed working with me.

"You have this critical eye, and when I say *critical*, I'm not tearing you down. I was thinking you're like a nurse in the critical care unit. Think about that. Every single decision they make is critical for a person to survive. You have that kind of critical eye, that everything you see is essential for us to move forward. The way you package it is nauseating because it makes everyone feel devalued who has worked hard on this project—the graphic artist, the engineers, and the music people."

"Honestly, Jill, that's not what I meant—"

"No one knows that better than I do. So from now on, I need you to tell me what's right before anything else."

To her credit, she did just that in our meetings. Tensions eased and others smiled in appreciation.

As we were leaving a meeting, I whispered, "Your limitation has now become a strength."

If You Are a C

- ▸ "Do it myself" is often your stance instead of allowing others to help.

- ▸ "Tell it like it is" is your mantra. You like to give everything straight, regardless of how hearers respond.

▸ You need to double-check or triple-check all your figures and findings.

▸ You acknowledge and appreciate yourself for being calm under pressure.

▸ You offer conservative approaches and avoid risk-taking.

▸ Explain to others that you're not difficult to please but that you have exacting standards and you do understand their reactions to them.

▸ A need for approval is high for you.

▸ Face the reality that your goals may be unrealistic because you're too meticulous.

▸ You experience little interaction with others. You're known as the solitary type.

▸ You are self-assured when you speak about projects and activities, but you're not good at expressing your feelings.

▸ You appreciate beautiful things. Typically, you're the person who stops to smell the roses.

Interacting with a C Style

▸ Be as specific as possible. Don't generalize.

▸ Think *quality control* as their base when you confront them.

▸ Recognizing and pointing out their loyalty and dedication is a good way to gain their attention.

▸ Acknowledge that their attention to detail makes them accurate statisticians and empathize when they want to spend an amazing amount of time correcting a minor detail or a phrase used in a proposal.

▶ Don't criticize or cause them to feel put down.

▶ Fearful of looking foolish, they will sometimes oppose new ideas or concepts in order to establish and protect their personal authority.

▶ Remind yourself that this person is an organizer; don't try to systemize for them.

▶ Honor their need to be alone.

▶ Respond to them in a reserved, even formal way unless they indicate otherwise.

▶ A C's normal reaction is to respond passively or aggressively to justify their actions.

▶ Be patient, persistent, and diplomatic, and provide explanations for your statements or position.

CHAPTER NINE

The Fear Factor

"Jill, I'm taking you to Paris," my husband said. I was beyond excited! My heart was overwhelmed at the thought of a romantic getaway. I had just begun mentally picking out my first travel outfit when Danny further clarified: "We are going to Paris, Tennessee."

What? Why? "A skydiving business there has an opening for me and a few of the guys to jump this afternoon."

We were in the middle of a series at church called Fear Factor. Danny had researched "top ten phobias." His intention was to bring awareness of fear and to equip and empower people to conquer their fears. For instance, the fear of spiders and snakes is a very real fear. My brilliant husband decided to go to a local pet store with our good friend, Joel. Joel took a video of Danny holding a snake while discussing the reality of ophidiophobia— the irrational fear of snakes. This served as a video opener to set up the sermon.

Aerophobia is the fear of flying that affects up to 40 percent of travelers. Acrophobia is the fear of heights that can cause severe anxiety attacks.

"We are going to capture a video of me and some of the guys jumping out of a plane, but Joel wants to jump as well, so I need you to come along to film the entire group."

"No problem," I thought.

As I walked from the living room to our bedroom to gather my things, I heard an inner voice say, "Get your tennis shoes. You are going to jump as well."

At first, I dismissed it. "Do you know me?" I started a very convincing dialogue with the invisible voice. No way was I jumping out of a perfectly safe, mechanically sound airplane. I am an S; safety, security, and stability all perfect descriptions of my characteristics. My D husband was all about taking the risk, but my S in no way stood for Skydiving.

In hopes that I could somehow forfeit this inner directive, I kept my mouth shut. One thing I know is that once you say you are going to do something, there will be others who will hold you accountable. I did not want the peer pressure of the guys on the trip to verbally push me into something I knew I was not wired to do. I'm not a risk-taker. Filming is one thing; you get to stay on the ground. Jumping is absolutely not an option.

A few hours later with several miles to go, the five guys and I were in a van on our way to Paris. The closer we got to the destination, the more I noticed the behavior of each one of the guys begin to shift. Nerves have a way of revealing each behavioral style under stress.

Billy, a High I, began to get more and more chatty. The closer we got, the more he talked.

Dave, Eric, and Joel, all having a combination of I and S, started making jokes. Their quick wit kept them bouncing off each other like a game of hacky sack. Their nervousness kept the atmosphere light with hilarious comedic relief. Danny, a D and a C, was going over the details for the video shoot, giving directions for different shots so we all knew what to do once we arrived. I was still silent. My facial expression was extremely focused on appearing relaxed as the internal debate inside my head was intensifying. I was slowly building a wall of self-preservation. The other passengers had no idea of my war within.

We arrived at the location, and the guys all went through the preparation process for the dive. I shrieked as we watched a video informing eager participants of the many risks involved. "We are not to be held liable for any injuries or sudden death. Sign here, please." No thank you. Not for me.

Instead of everyone going up at once and jumping out of the plane one after the other, we were informed that we had to go up one at a time and jump in tandem with the instructor. Waiting my turn gave me just enough time for the inner voice to talk me into doing the jump.

I was halfway through explaining to Joel that "I think I'm going to jump" when I felt my body slowly succumb to a paralyzing fear. The coming blackout was suddenly interrupted. "This is incredible!" Joel exclaimed. "Everyone expects Danny to do something like this, but no one will ever believe that you would jump." All of a sudden, I knew I had just committed myself and there was no backing out. What had I done?

Deep inside, I knew the inner voice was the voice of God helping me to conquer one of my greatest fears so that I could rise above the limitation I had placed on myself. My future was being held hostage by my need for security. Opportunities had been knocking at my door, but I had been too afraid to open it. My self-critical mind monsters kept taunting me with reasons why I was inadequate to move forward.

The moment I stepped out of that perfectly safe, mechanically sound airplane and jumped into the sky, something broke off me. "The sky's the limit!" became a reality. My body was strapped to the instructor. My entire life was at the mercy of his hands. All of a sudden, the inner voice began to affirm me. "You did it, you trusted me; your faith in how I wired you is greater than your fear of failure." The next thing I heard would change my life forever.

"Because you trusted me, I can now trust you."

As soon as I felt the parachute open, I felt a peace overwhelm me. *I'm in good hands,* I thought to myself. And I'm not just referring to the instructor.

Fear and faith are both powerful emotions. I've heard it said, "Faith is believing that what you cannot see will come to pass." I may not be able to see what I hope for with my eyes, but I can see it with my heart. In addition, I've heard, "Fear is also believing what you cannot see will come to pass." A Japanese proverb states, "Fear is only as deep as the mind allows."

Childhood fears take rational appearances and distort them into irrational monsters, ready to pounce. As children, we've all had some kind of "monster under the bed" scenario. It's tragic when the monster under the bed grows up with an adult and becomes the monster in the mind. Especially when the mind monster wreaks havoc by distorting our perception of life through a lens of fear. This lens often unleashes a behavior that is destructive. You can either continue going in the same direction and allow fear to dominate your path, or you can decide to disarm that fear by kicking it out of the driver's seat and take back control of your life.

"We are more often frightened than hurt; and we suffer more from imagination than from reality" (Seneca the Elder, ancient Roman writer).

Fear manipulates our imagination to expect the worst. When we imagine the worst, our behavior is appropriately affected. Living in fear leads to behaving in fear. This can cause devastating distortion to our relationships and opportunities. Our *perceived* reality becomes our reality.

Each one of the behaviors has a dominant fear. I mentioned these in the previous chapters, but for the sake of clarity, here they are:

Dominant Fears

- ▶ The D: Being taken advantage of
- ▶ The I: Rejection
- ▶ The S: Loss of security
- ▶ The C: Criticism

It's human nature to protect oneself when feeling attacked or threatened. When motivated by fear, each style of behavior will express itself accordingly.

Ds will self-protect with aggression. If they feel loss of control, they will overcompensate by intensifying demands and barking orders.

When faced with the fear of rejection, the I style will dominate the conversation. They will find the center of the stage and put themselves right in the spotlight. The word *I* becomes the topic of conversation as they desperately search for affirmation.

The S style will lock themselves up in a will of iron. They go silent but remain extremely stubborn. Change may mean a loss of security, so they often resist it. They strive to find a place of stability.

Criticism is the greatest fear of the C. Pointing out the faults in others makes their own failures seem palatable. They fend for themselves by pushing others away with their negativity and mood swings. When fear strikes, they seek correctness.

We live in a society where fear is a tactic used by media to manipulate control. Thus, we feel that crises—real or imagined—are all around us. Our response to crises will determine their impact in our life.

In my fifty years of living, I have never experienced a global shutdown. In the first quarter of 2020, the world as we knew it was forever changed by an invisible virus known as COVID-19. This pandemic has swept our nation and all other nations of the world. In an attempt to contain the spread of the virus, people all over the globe were mandated to self-quarantine.

Only a limited amount of businesses and organizations were acknowledged as "essential," allowing them to remain open. Homes became schools and parents became teachers in order to maintain education. The music and entertainment industry completely shut down as public events and gatherings became a threat to spreading the virus. Churches were forced to reinvent themselves to online experiences only. Some transformed into testing centers for the virus as well as food donation centers for those in need. Hospitals had to reschedule surgeries and make room for the anticipated virus victims. Doctors and nurses, first responders, and all those maintaining the essentials, put their own health at risk just by showing up to work each day.

Face masks were mandated to be worn. Hand sanitizer and cleaning supplies were in high demand. People were seen fighting over a pack of toilet paper.

This pandemic literally changed the way of life for billions of people.

As governors and city mayors worked together to reopen their territories, another crisis erupted in America. On May 25, 2020, George Floyd, a forty-six-year-old Black man, was killed in Minneapolis, Minnesota, during an arrest for allegedly using a counterfeit bill. A White police officer, Derek Chauvin, knelt on Floyd's neck for several minutes while Floyd was facedown lying on the ground, handcuffed and begging for his life. Video clips of him saying, "I can't breathe!" went viral, and people of all races became enraged. The autopsy of Floyd confirmed his death a homicide. My heart was grieved as I watched the images of one man taking the life of another man. "He is not an animal!" I screamed. "He is a human being!" I was completely vexed and angered. And I was not alone in my sentiment.

George Floyd's death unleashed a movement all across America of protests, marches, and demonstrations.

Black men and women have suffered for centuries from racism and White advantage. I live in Franklin, Tennessee. There are plaques and historical markers all throughout this town identifying it as the location of the bloodiest battle in the Civil War. Cannonballs from the war were found right up the street from where I live.

Are we still dealing with this? my heart cried as the news filled the airwaves and social media. I could almost hear the blood begin to cry out from the soldiers' graves: "We already gave our lives for freedom. Why are we still dealing with this? When will this injustice cease?"

Even though there had been countless injustices to people of color in the past, there was something different about this tragedy. In the midst of pain and division, there was a unity arising. Could this truly be the beginning of change?

In my hopefulness, I began to notice the variety of responses to the state of our nation. The more I sorted through reactions, the more I became aware that different styles of behavior respond differently in times of crisis. As I begin to unpack this revelation, remember the four categories of dominant behavior that I have identified in this book. DISC is the code of identification for these dominant styles. For more than two decades I have profiled, assessed, and consulted the behavior of thousands of people. It is rare that a person is a pure breed. "Pure breed" refers to the person who only has one behavioral style. This is very rare. Most people have a combination of styles. For instance, I am an SIC. My S is dominant, but I also express the characteristics of an I and a C. I find that the descriptions and characteristics of each of these styles reflect that of my own. However, certain environments bring out the different styles of the combinations of behavior.

Unpacking all the different combinations and their strengths and limitations would be laborious. Understanding the strengths and limitations of each of these styles will empower you to recognize their characteristics in your own personal combination of behavior. This is vital to understanding why you or others respond to crisis the way you do.

I noticed that during the coronavirus pandemic, certain people were very intentional about wearing their masks, while others walked around the grocery store as if nothing was happening.

In an environment of choice, with the option to wear a mask, it became evident that the dominant D wanted to remain in control. Wearing a mask would be the result of them choosing to wear it. Being forced to wear a mask only served to take away their freedom.

The dominant I style most likely didn't wear a mask unless it had some fun pattern or material that caused them to stand out. Even with this prerequisite, they couldn't wear the mask for too long because it impeded their ability to talk freely and greatly impaired their ability to be sociable. They also weren't found wearing masks because, honestly, they just forgot to bring one.

Now, the dominant S style wore masks most of the time to follow the rules, thereby avoiding confrontation or conflict. Remember, they just "go with the flow" and do whatever keeps the peace. They most likely carried extra masks to freely give to those who were without.

The dominant C would not be seen without a mask. They are also a rule follower. Their motivation for following the rules was to keep them correct. They not only followed the rules, they also memorized them. They, too, had extra masks to share but may have wanted them returned after use.

The D and I are both extroverts, so they deeply struggled with the act of self-quarantine. FaceTime calls and Zoom meetings became their oxygen. Staying productive was the only way for a D to get through it. Staying socially connected was the way for an I to survive. Without some type of outlet for these extroverts, they would sink into a deep depression. They would even bend the rules to meet deadlines or meet up with others.

S and C introverts were less likely to go out in public. Especially until the officials of their cities gave the green light. They did not want to break the rules. The S style most likely found themselves on numerous calls from friends and family, listening to their concerns and giving them a peaceful, comforting response. The Cs were full of information, updating others with stats and percentages and formulating plans. They could recite their governors' executive orders for reopening their states and would make sure others followed suit.

The Ds and Cs most likely had a pantry stocked with supplies, ready for worst-case scenarios. The I and S styles were more concerned about checking on their loved ones.

Please understand this: We can focus on the differences of each style and make them an issue, or we can choose to see the best in each other. If we notice the strengths of each behavioral style, we will quickly understand that we truly are better together.

During the protests, I noticed that some were very vocal while others seemed to shut down. "We need your voice" became a common cry from all races. "We must not stay silent." Yet so many found themselves speechless, not knowing what to say. The more I pondered and studied the different responses, it made sense to me why the extroverted D and I styles were so vocal while the S and C styles were slow to open their mouths.

In my opinion, it's vital to seek understanding before you seek to be understood, especially in crisis situations. To only seek to be understood postures a self-righteous attitude that brings division. People are wired differently. They do not all respond the same, especially in the middle of an uprising. To assume their silence is betrayal is not always a fair assumption.

For some, silence is just hesitation. An S is hesitant to speak up because he or she is not wired for conflict. The S style struggles internally for the right thing to say. Not because they need to be right but because they don't like to make others feel wrong. Their supreme passion for peace will hijack their voice. They wrestle eternally with the thought of saying the wrong thing and hurting others.

The Cs remains silent until they have gathered all the facts and data. Researching the history, reading the different reports, and assessing the truth are essential to stating their case or lending their voice. They hesitate to speak up until they are fully convinced that they are speaking the truth based on facts. They struggle with the right thing to say because they need to be right. The thought of speaking up and making themselves look foolish motivates them to remain silent.

Both the S and C styles will eventually speak up and march for the cause. Once they believe in something, they become great supporters. They just take a bit more time and preparation for action.

Ds have no problem speaking up. In fact, they do so with charisma and persuasive conviction. They will risk it all for the sake of the cause. Their self-confidence is both admirable and overwhelming. The dominant D is the first to speak up, lead the protest, and take charge. The thought of speaking up doesn't concern them at all. They must speak the truth, even if it causes a riot. Their determination is unstoppable.

The I style is the cheerleader. They, too, have no issue with speaking up. They will shout the loudest and the longest. They are masters at motivating others. If not careful, they can draw more attention to themselves than to the cause. They long to be a part of the action. They don't always know what to do, but they definitely want to align themselves with those who do know what to do.

In seasons of crisis, it's important to understand that our differences do not have to be a source of division. In reality, our differences are a source of great strength.

CHAPTER **TEN**

The Arena
of Trust

A major task I face in helping clients develop and overcome their limitations is to enable them to recognize their blind spots. And we all have them. But there's a reason they're called *blind* spots.

In his book, *The Invisible Gorilla,* Dr. Daniel Simons discusses an experiment he conducted in 1999. In his experiment, Simons showed volunteers a video of two teams of three people each. One team wore black, the other white. The six players were in the center of the screen and their facial expressions close enough to be clearly seen. Each team had its own basketball. In the video, they bounced it or threw it to their own teammates as they moved and feinted in the small space where the game was filmed.

Before showing the video to the group of volunteers, Dr. Simons asked them to watch closely and to count the number of times the white shirts threw the ball to each other. After a few minutes, he stopped the video and asked them to report the number of passes.

"Fifteen!"

"Correct!"

They smiled, pleased they had passed the test. Then he asked, "Did you see the gorilla?"

Someone laughed. At first, most of them thought he was joking. "There was no gorilla in the picture," they all agreed.

"Watch the video again," said Simons, "but this time, don't count."

About a minute into the video, a man dressed in a gorilla suit walked up the middle of the court and beat his chest.

This time every one of them saw the animal—but then, they were looking for it.

You, like all of us, focus on the moving basketball. Consequently, you miss other things—important things. The decision to move forward in a relationship, for instance, where you just don't see the other person's true colors. Yet those you trust— your family, your friends—can see right through their intentions. "Blinded by love" is a term often used to describe a person who refuses to see the limitations or faults in their potential life partner. Understanding how you are wired is key to recognizing that we all have blind spots. That's where the DISC profile can come in handy. Knowing your natural limitations empowers you to choose awareness and then choose to change your behavior.

You don't know what you don't know. Sounds simple, yet it is so profound in describing a blind spot. A blind spot is when you don't see what you don't see. The challenge is that others do see what you don't see. A willingness to ask or be receptive to feedback can remove the blind spots preventing you from making progress in your relationships or job.

Have you ever left a group conversation feeling confident that you made a great first impression until that ghastly moment you catch your reflection in a window or mirror, only to see a rogue piece of pepper lodged in the middle of your top center front teeth? *How long has this been here?* you think. *Why didn't anyone say anything?* If you are a D or an I, you might feel a quick sense of embarrassment but then return to the group, laughing it all off and blaming the chef. If you are an S or C, you quickly find the nearest exit and leave feeling very insecure.

Blind spots can leave us feeling very vulnerable once they are exposed. This can lead to a deep sense of distrust between spouses, family members, and team members. Without a sense of trust, it is very difficult to see progress. Trust equity is vital to increasing value in any relationship. To experience success in our interactions with others, we must operate in the arena of trust.

Perception determines reception. How others perceive you determines how they will receive you. Likewise, how you perceive others will determine how you will receive them.

Let's look at an example. A particular office asked me to come investigate the source of division impeding their progress on a simple project.

"She's just out for my job," Darcy exclaimed. "She's not really interested in helping me; she wants to take all the credit for the work I have done."

Darcy, a High D, was notorious for pushing others out of her group projects. Why? Because she perceived they were just going to take advantage of all her hard work. Darcy wanted to get full credit for her job well done. Yet her deep misperception of her team was about to greatly cost her and her team. How could they move forward together without trusting each other?

"This is a team project," I replied. "Why do you have such distrust in this team?" Darcy looked at me with deep sorrow in her eyes and began to explain.

"In my last job," she began, "I did all the work for a major commercial real estate project. It was a two-year project."

I already began to see the handwriting on the wall.

"In the end," she said, "I was let go because my teammate blindsided me by hiding secret information that prevented me from making vital decisions. The project was sabotaged."

Darcy had walked on this current team with a predisposed lack of trust for others. She filtered her new teammates through the pain and betrayal of her last team. It was evident to me that Darcy needed to learn to trust again before this team would ever see success.

In 1955, American psychologists Joseph Luft and Harry Ingham developed a model to better enhance understanding and communication between others in a group setting. This model is known as the Johari Window. The name "Johari" came from joining their first names.

The window model is used to enhance the individual's perception of others. This model is based on two ideas. First, trust can be acquired by revealing information about you to others. Second, you can learn more about yourself from the feedback of others. There are four quadrants, or "windowpanes," that represent how we communicate with ourselves and with others. Each of the four panes signify personal information, feelings, and motivation.

They identify whether that information is known or unknown to oneself or others in the four viewpoints shown in the model.

Open arena of trust (I know and You know)	Blind Spot (You know, I don't know)
Mask (I know, You don't know)	Unknown (I don't know, You don't know)

How we both convey and accept feedback is interpreted in this model. The idea is that in order to operate or move into the arena of trust, there must be an exchange of information through socializing. Sharing information about oneself and receiving the feedback from group members will move the participants from the unknown into an arena of mutual trust.

The unknown area is what you and others are unaware of. This includes information, feelings, talents, capabilities, etc. Trauma or past experiences may have locked away the ability to see what is there. Without the discovery of these hidden qualities or observations, the unknown could last a lifetime. Open communication and the willingness to allow others to speak into your life will decrease the unknown area and increase mutual trust.

When you are unaware of information about yourself, yet others are aware, this is the blind spot I referred to previously. This area can be reduced for better communication by seeking feedback from others.

Information that is known to you but is unknown to others is the area we call the mask.

In the ancient Greek tragedy plays, actors held up happy or sad masks in front of their faces. They called the actors *hupokrites*, which transliterates into the English word *hypocrites*. These actors were expressing emotions that they realized were not their own. That's why hypocrite is a word that refers to a pretender or someone who speaks words while inwardly knowing they're lying.

Ten times in Matthew's Gospel, Jesus called the Jewish leaders hypocrites—the most scathing rebuke in the New Testament. Although they wouldn't admit it, those leaders knew they were dishonest. If they hadn't known, we could say they had blind spots. But by Jesus using that word, He pointed out the evil in their hearts, declaring they knew; therefore, we know they were choosing to wear masks.

Probably the most difficult part in working with clients is to get them to take off their masks—which are usually there for self-protection. In his book, *Twelve Rules for Life: An Antidote to Chaos,* Jordan Peterson, a world-renowned therapist, wrote this about himself: "I . . . came to realize that almost everything I said was untrue. I had motives for saying these things: I wanted to win arguments and gain status and impress people and get what I wanted. I was using language to bend and twist the world into delivering what I thought was necessary. But I was a fake."

You may not be able to be honest with yourself or others just yet, but you can set yourself on the pathway toward unmasking. It demands courage to discard your mask and let others see your wrinkles and observe your foibles.

God knows who you are—everything about you—and still loves you. Like many others, you may be afraid that if you reveal who you truly are, people won't like you. And this is a risk you have to take.

Wouldn't you rather be a person of whom people say, "He's the real deal"? Or "What you see is what you get"? Author Cecil Murphey has a saying: "I'd rather be disliked for who I am than to be admired for who I'm not."

The open arena of trust is the goal. This is where the information about the person and their attitudes, behaviors, emotions, feelings, skills, and views will be known by all parties involved. The most effective communication takes place in this quadrant. Blind spots are exposed and masks are not permitted to enter. This is where relationships are strong and success unstoppable. This is where all behavioral styles excel.

Let's go back to Darcy. The success of her new job and position required mutual trust. Moving from the unknown quadrant first required Darcy to remove her mask. After gathering the group together, I encouraged Darcy to share her previous experience, thus revealing that her distrust was justified. Sharing information that only she knew released understanding in the others; they could see why Darcy was hesitant to share relevant information. Their suspicion quickly turned to compassion. Revealing the truth in a situation may seem like a risk, but it's a risk worth taking.

The very thing Darcy was trying to conceal became the key to unlock compassion in the others. They didn't judge her for getting fired from her previous job like she had feared. Instead, a surge of camaraderie flooded the room, and the project moved forward with all participating. The result was a success—both in the short term (the project itself) and the long term. Trust among the team members continued to grow, leading to even more success. But this level of trust didn't come immediately. It took much more work.

In my experience, staying in the quadrant of revealing what is behind the mask can increase a sense of victimization. Endless replies of, "Sorry for your loss," and, "But we aren't that team," would just keep us on a merry-go-round of apologies. We still had to move along and get Darcy and her team into that place of mutual trust. To keep things rolling, I then had to facilitate the feedback coming from the other team members to Darcy.

"Darcy, you are a brilliant team leader," Renee quickly shared. "We are all here to help assist you with our different skills; however, we are often pushed aside by your lack of instruction and clarity. Your invisible wall often takes too much energy to climb over, so we sit outside your protective kingdom waiting for you to lower the drawbridge allowing us inside."

I looked over at Darcy. She was not yet convinced of her job security, but there was a shred of light breaking through the dark threat of fear holding her hostage. One by one, the team assured Darcy that they were not after her job. She began to listen to their feedback, and over time we had a successful mission. This exercise and interaction landed all five members of the group on the island of trust. Now they could move forward together celebrating each one's contribution with mutual trust and respect.

Recognizing Darcy as a High D also revealed to me her greatest fear: being taken advantage of. This was confirmed by her exclamation that her coworker was just out to get her job. Now combining this information on her behavioral style with the Johari Window, I was able to identify the limitation of the entire group and bring resolution through effective communication, relocating them from the unknown to the arena of trust.

The Johari Window is a great tool to strengthen any relation-ship. Marriages that were once in shambles suddenly come to a place of mutual trust when the masks are removed and the blind spots revealed. Families are reunited when willing to sit down and walk through this exercise. Understanding how a person is wired helps remove the blind spots and enables them to see a little more clearly who they are. The limitations of each behavioral style are only limiting if they are tolerated through lack of recognition or denial. Awareness—self-awareness and the awareness by others—is key to healing. As painful as it may seem, they need to be aware of the gorilla in their midst—in their minds and hearts. And the blind spots aren't always negative. I often am able to point to good qualities and natural talents of which they were unaware.

Years ago, Skip volunteered to teach a teens' Bible study for a local church. He had the desire yet lacked the skills necessary for success at this task. He fumbled for words, couldn't seem to make the lesson relevant, and left the kids bored. However, the man in charge of Bible studies at the church saw something in Skip and said, "You're a great organizer. You'd do well as an administrator for all our study groups."

A shocked Skip agreed to try. And he did an outstanding job in this role—even though he was unaware that he had such talent. Oftentimes we are so focused on trying to do something we are not wired to do, we fail to see our own natural abilities and strengths. Being open to feedback is key to overcoming the bruises from tripping over your blind spots. But receiving that feedback often requires a level of trust. If someone is jealous of your promotion, they may not give you honest observations. Find those you like, love, and trust, and ask them to give you their honest evaluation. You may be surprised to find that what you think is just an ordinary gift or talent is actually extraordinary in the eyes of others.

CHAPTER ELEVEN

Taking Shape

It can be quite humorous watching a baby feverishly attempting to force a round block into a triangular space in a shape-sorting toy. What began with a hopeful smile ends in tears of frustration. The daunting sense of hopelessness and failure is suddenly dismissed by the simple turning of the ball and the pointing of a parent directing their little fingers to the appropriate space. The round block has finally found the round space, a perfect fit. The parent cheers and the baby smiles. The celebration is short lived as the baby picks up the triangular block and begins to feverishly force it into the square space. The repetitive game keeps the baby entertained and the parent hopeful that, through experience, the baby will begin to recognize which space is reserved for each specific shape.

Surprisingly, I've seen this same frustration expressed on the faces of many others throughout the years: People with unspoken expectations who constantly find themselves disappointed when those expectations are left unmet. Wives who try to force their introverted husbands to join them on a company vacation. Parents who put their shy and insecure child on the spot by asking them to perform on cue as if to affirm their parental skills. Employers who confine their extroverted employee to a cubicle focusing on charts and data, instead of creating space for them to find their perfect fit interacting with others. Volunteers who fail to show up because they were never given clear expectations or details, leaving a stressed leader trying to fill their vacant spaces.

Trying to force yourself to take on the shape you think others expect you to be can also be an endless cycle of defeat.

In every story, there is a common denominator of a need to understand yourself and others. *Misunderstanding* leads to misdirection and malfunction, while *understanding* leads to empowerment and unity. Recognizing your own strengths and limitations—the way you are wired—will equip you to make good choices. Behavior can be chosen, not just inherited. We all need each other, but we benefit from the best version of each of the DISC behavioral styles. And let's be honest, we sleep better knowing we did our part.

Like any pattern in our lives, behavior is built or broken by consistency. According to Healthline, a website for health topics, it takes an average of sixty-six days for a new behavior to become automatic. This makes me think of my first car.

I'll never forget opening the door to my blue, two-door, previously owned Honda Civic. It looked like a roller skate. I could not wait to get a job and start working. Earning my own money was at the top of my list. At this stage of my life, both my parents worked. I, too, wanted to bring home the bacon, so to speak. And in order to work, I needed transportation. So, the blue Civic was key to my gaining independence and acquiring a strong work ethic.

When I opened the door, my excitement turned to terror as I saw this "stick" in the middle of the car. It was a stick shift—my car had a five-speed manual transmission. This meant I had to learn how to put my left foot on the clutch while in neutral, turn the ignition key, take my left foot off the clutch, and press the brake with my right foot. Each time I shifted gears beginning with first, I had to basically choreograph my left and right feet to navigate accordingly. Left foot on the clutch, shift the gear, lifting off the pressure from the left foot and slowly increasing the accelerator with my right. In the beginning it was a nightmare; knowing when to shift gears, how much pressure to put on which of the three pedals under my feet. It's exhausting just recounting the memories.

And just as I would get the hang of things, the worst would happen. I would end up at stop sign that was perfectly placed at the top of a hill.

For those of you who have no idea what this means, balancing the clutch and the accelerator could mean the difference between moving forward after a complete stop or rolling backward, hitting the person stopped behind you. This was genuine pressure.

My entire body was under complete stress every time I turned the ignition key. Balancing the transmission, keeping my eyes alert, and maintaining safety required every ounce of focus and energy. "You'll get the hang of it, just keep driving," my dad would say. "It will get easier and easier the more you do it."

For the first several months, I cussed and prayed more than I ever had in my life. (I will say that the prayers definitely seemed more effective than the profanity.) Eventually, and to my surprise, my dad's theory was correct. Consistency had finally paid off. I'll never forget the moment I turned on the car's radio to actually enjoy the music instead of an attempt to drown out my random outbursts.

Much like driving my first car, changing behavior may seem impossible. Let me encourage you that although it may require your total focus and energy in the beginning, your consistency will pay off. Just keep going. You'll get the hang of it. Soon your behavior will shift into automatic and you will enjoy the symphony of life.

I want to leave you with one last thought. God wired you in a specific way. To live the way He has made you honors Him greatly. Yet, for some reason, so many of us try to live and think and act in a way for which we weren't wired. To do so is dishonoring to God. It is us basically saying to the Creator, "You didn't know what You were doing, so now I'll take over." And that leads to disaster every time.

Thus, it is vital to learn just how we are wired and then learn how to live the way we were made to live. I hope I've shown you how the DISC assessment tool is a great way to learn just how you are wired. I want you to know your wonderful strengths. I want you to see your limitations not as flaws but as areas of your life where you can lean on the strengths in others. We are not meant to journey in life by ourselves. Together, we are much greater.

Here is my final word for you. I recommend you memorize this so you can call it to mind often. This was written by Gordon MacKenzie, who served as the creative director for Hallmark for almost thirty years. He learned by experience that artists often become smothered in a corporation and end up in a cubicle creating art not from their hearts but from a memo written by a nonartist. The artist loses the desire to create—a desire that produces energy and vitality carried over in all aspects of their life—and tries to be someone else in order to fit in. MacKenzie was so adamantly against this that he wrote *Orbiting the Giant Hairball* to encourage each of us to live just as we are wired to live.

This is how he concludes his book:

"You have a masterpiece inside you, you know. One unlike any that has ever been created, or ever will be. If you go to your grave without painting your masterpiece, it will not get painted. No one else can paint it. Only you."

Now, get out your brush and canvas, and paint your masterpiece.

EPILOGUE

On September 23, 2020, shortly after this book was written, my Happily Ever After and best friend, Danny Chambers, took his last breath on earth. He was my forever cheerleader and believed greatly in this book. His encouragement and support were the wind beneath my wings that allowed this dream to become a reality. The stories and principles in this book are moments and memories that we will forever share. His passing came before its completion, leaving me feeling deeply sorrowful, yet I know he is proud. His eyes may not experience reading these words from an earthly point of view, but his spirit is watching over me, and I feel his smile and congratulations.

I love and miss you Danny, ferociously and forever.

AUTHOR CONTACT

If you would like to contact Jill Chambers, find out more information, purchase books, or request her to speak, please contact:

Jill Chambers

jillchambers.com

instagram.com/jillianchambers

facebook.com/jillchamberscoach

ABOUT THE AUTHOR

Jill Chambers has a humanitarian heart that beats for justice. Her fierce passion leads her all over the world, creating awareness to the social injustice of human trafficking and bringing resources to the impoverished and hope to those in need. She travels and speaks worldwide to multiracial and multigenerational audiences.

As a keynote speaker, educator, and life coach, Jill has been training people in leadership skills under the headship of the John C. Maxwell organization for over two decades.

She has spent the last twenty years training people in behavioral science in the marketplace and in churches all over the world. She is a highly trained teacher and communicator using PeopleKeys to educate and help individuals understand their value as well as appreciate others and their differences.

Helping people understand their value and training them to make strong life choices is essential to Jill's own personal mission. A founding pastor for twenty-two years, she has invested in the lives of thousands of people globally. With singing, modeling, and television production in her background, she communicates with humor and an authentic love for her audience. Connecting people to their Creator so they can discover the value of their uniqueness has produced tremendous change in the way men and women of all ages value themselves.

This year marks the thirty-first wedding anniversary of Jill to her late husband, Danny. She is the proud mother of five amazing children, mother-in-law to four amazing "in-loves," and "Honey" to eight grandchildren.